A SCRIPTURAL CATECHISM

Expanded Edition

Fr. Herbert Burke

Foreword by
Bishop Peter J. Jugis

**A HELPFUL RESOURCE FOR
R.C.I.A. AND C.C.D. or FAITH FORMATION PROGRAMS**

**FULLY INDEXED TO THE
"CATECHISM OF THE CATHOLIC CHURCH"**

A SCRIPTURAL CATECHISM

Expanded Edition

Fr. Herbert Burke

Foreword by Bishop Peter J. Jugis

**A HELPFUL RESOURCE FOR
R.C.I.A. AND C.C.D. or FAITH FORMATION PROGRAMS**

**FULLY INDEXED TO THE
"CATECHISM OF THE CATHOLIC CHURCH"**

PUBLISHING COMPANY
P.O. Box 220 • Goleta, CA 93116
(800) 647-9882 • (805) 692-0043 • Fax: (805) 967-5133
www.queenship.org

✝

Nihil Obstat:
Abbot Placid Solari, O.S.B., S.T.D.
Censor Deputatus

Imprimatur:
Most Reverend Peter J. Jugis, J.C.D.
Bishop of Charlotte

October 7, 2005

The nihil obstat and imprimatur are official declarations that a book or pamphlet is free of doctrinal or moral error. No implication is contained therein that those who have granted the nihil obstat and the imprimatur agree with the content, opinions or statements expressed.

Library of Congress Number #2006903351
Published by:
Queenship Publishing
P.O. Box 220
Goleta, CA 93116
800-647-9882 • 805-692-0043 • Fax 805-967-5155
www.queenship.org

Printed in the United states of America

ISBN:1-57918-298-4

Written in Honor of Mary,
Queen of the Most Holy Rosary

Table of Contents

Part II
The Seven Sacraments

Part III
The Commandments

Part IV
Prayer

Foreword

"There is nothing more beautiful than to be surprised by the Gospel, by the encounter with Christ. There is nothing more beautiful than to know Him and to speak to others of our friendship with Him." Pope Benedict XVI spoke these words on April 24, 2005 at the Mass inaugurating his ministry as supreme pastor of the Church. In a few words, the Holy Father captured the beauty and the essence of the Christian life: to encounter the living Christ, to know him and love Him, and to live in friendship with Him, sharing His truth and love with others.

The present book helps the reader to grow in the knowledge of the Catholic faith, and thereby to know and love better the one who is the author of faith. As the title of the books suggests, the unique contribution of *A Scriptural Catechism* is to provide the scriptural basis for the beliefs and practices of the Catholic Church. It seeks to unite the basic teachings of the Church on the creed, the sacraments, the commandments and prayer, with scripture quotations, references and practical reasons. Thus the reader is able to see the harmony between Catholic beliefs and sacred scripture.

The Second Vatican Council encouraged all the Christian faithful to "learn 'the surpassing knowledge of Jesus Christ'(Phil. 3:8) by frequent reading of the divine scriptures. 'Ignorance of the Scriptures is ignorance of Christ.'" (Dogmatic Constitution on Divine Revelation *Dei Verbum*, n. 25). Instruction in the faith is greatly enriched by being joined to a study of sacred Scripture. The present catechism, with its numerous references to Scripture, keeps the reader in constant contact with the divine Word, and leads the reader to a richer understanding of the content of faith.

A Scriptural Catechism is fully indexed to the *Catechism of the Catholic Church*. The reader is able to use the present book as a bridge to learn more about each subject from the official catechism, which is "a sure and authentic reference text for teaching catholic doctrine and particularly for preparing local catechisms." (Pope John Paul II, Apostolic constitution *Fidei Depositum*, October 11, 1992: paragraph 21). This book is a useful resource for RCIA programs, faith formation programs, youth groups, and Catholics who want a quick review of their faith. It is also a useful took for religious educators, priests, religious and all involved in education and evangelization.

May this catechism contribute to the spread of the Gospel and the salvation of souls. May it inspire the reader to grow in friendship with Christ, and to share the Lord's love and truth with others.

Most Reverend Peter J. Jugis
Bishop of Charlotte

Part I

The Creed

"Jesus said to her, 'I am the resurrection and the life; he who believes in me, though he die, yet shall he live, and whoever lives and believes in me shall never die.'" (Jn. 11:25, 26)

What is the Purpose of Life?
[Cross Reference:1-3, 1718, Catechism of the Catholic Church]

We were created to be perfectly happy forever with God. Perfect happiness can only be found in perfect life, love, and truth, which is God. *"I have no good apart from thee"* (Ps.16).

True and perfect happiness does not consist in temporary and imperfect, material possessions,

...a man's life does not consist in the abundance of his possessions. (Lk. 12:15) For what does it profit a man, if he gain the whole world, and suffer the loss of his own soul? (Mt. 16:26)

sensual pleasures,

...the eye is not satisfied with seeing, nor the ear filled with hearing. (Ec. 1:8)

and human friendships, *He who loves father or mother more than me is not worthy of me...* (Mt. 10:37), *For in the resurrection they neither marry...but are like angels in heaven.* (Mt. 22:30, Also: 1 Cor. 7:29),

but, only in perfect and eternal friendship with God. This perfect union with God begins in this world and is completed in heaven.

St. Augustine: "You have made us for yourself, O Lord, and our hearts are restless until they rest in you."

"Do not lay up for yourselves treasures on earth, where moth and rust consume and where thieves break in and steal, but lay up for yourselves treasures in heaven, where neither moth nor rust consumes and where thieves do not break in and steal. For where your treasure is, there will your heart be also. Therefore do not be anxious, saying, 'What shall we eat?' or 'What shall we drink?' or 'What shall we wear?' For the Gentiles [Unbelievers] seek all these things; and your heavenly Father knows that you need them all. **But seek first his kingdom and his righteousness,** and all these things shall be yours as well. (Mt. 6:19-21, 31-33)

The purpose of life is to love God and your neighbor (Mt. 22:37-39) through the 10 commandments (Mt. 19:17-19), the works of mercy (Mt. 25:31-46), and the 7 sacraments (Mk. 16:16, Jn.6:53). *"The Love of God consists in this: that we keep his commandments..."* (1 Jn. 5:3) This life is a test to see if we truly love God (Mt. 25:14-30).

"You have been told, O man, what is good, and what the Lord requires of you; only to do the right and to love goodness, and to walk humbly with your God." (Mic. 6:8)

How do I Know God Exists?
[31-38]

We know God exists through the things He has made. *"Since the creation of the world his invisible attributes are clearly seen—his everlasting power also and divinity—being understood through the things that are made."* (Rom. 1:20) Often the reason people reject God's existence is not based on logic, but on passion. They do not want to believe in God because this would mean they would have to keep His commandments. St.Augustine says: "He who denies the existence of God, has some reason for wishing that God did not exist." Natural theology is the knowledge of God we acquire through nature and reason.

We can know God exists through reason, not by seeing God Himself, but by seeing His effects, His creation. The traces of perfection we see in nature point to a Perfect Being Who caused all these traces of perfection. This is why the scripture says: *"From the greatness and the beauty of created things their original author, by analogy, is seen."* (Wis. 13:1-9) A hunter in the forest was once asked how he knew there is a God. He said, "In the same way I know by the footprints on the forest floor that a bear or deer has passed by, so too can I see from the marks of the world the fingerprints of God." If there was a Big Bang, who pulled the trigger? Every cause has an effect, and there cannot be a limitless number of limited causes because ultimately there must be an uncaused cause. If we have a line of dominoes and they fall down, something must have pushed the first one. God is the Uncaused Cause, the Unmoved Mover (cause and effect argument).

A Catholic and an atheist worked together in a car factory. The Catholic said, "Isn't it great that our new car came together by accident?" The atheist protested, "What do you mean, accident? There are many years of research, design, computers, and craftsmanship built into that car." The Catholic said, "Then by what logic do you conclude that the universe, which is much more intricate and ordered, came together by accident?" The intelligence of the design points to the intelligence of the designer. Science shows us the advanced design of the universe which points to an advanced designer - namely God. (Teleological Arg.)

How Can We experience God?
[2558-2565]

By opening our hearts in prayer and asking for His Holy Spirit to come into our heart and life, and by turning our backs on sin *"If you, evil as you are, know how to give good gifts to your children, how much more will your heavenly Father give the Good Spirit to those who ask him!"* (Lk. 11:13). *"Draw near to God, and he will draw near to you."* (Jam. 4:8) *"Behold, I stand at the door and knock. If any man listens to my voice and opens the door to me, I will come in to him and will sup with him, and he with me."* (Rev. 3:20)

What blocks us from Experiencing God?

An evil or selfish heart which turns away from God and toward the temptations, cares, riches and pleasures of life is what blocks us from experiencing and following God. The root of sin lies in bad choices made in the heart; Jesus said: "*For out of the heart come evil thoughts, murder, adultery, fornication, theft, false witness, slander. These are what defile a man.*" (Mt. 15:19-20)

This parable is the spiritual biography of everyone:

> And when a great crowd came together and people from town after town came to him, he said in a parable: {5} "A sower went out to sow his seed; and as he sowed, some fell along the path, and was trodden under foot, and the birds of the air devoured it. {6} And some fell on the rock; and as it grew up, it withered away, because it had no moisture. {7} And some fell among thorns; and the thorns grew with it and choked it. {8} And some fell into good soil and grew, and yielded a hundredfold." As he said this, he called out, "He who has ears to hear, let him hear." {9} And when his disciples asked him what this parable meant, {10} he said, "To you it has been given to know the secrets of the kingdom of God; but for others they are in parables, so that seeing they may not see, and hearing they may not understand. {11} Now the parable is this: The seed is the word of God. {12} The ones along the path are those who have heard; then the devil comes and takes away the word from their hearts, that they may not believe and be saved. {13} And the ones on the rock are those who, when they hear the word, receive it with joy; but these have no root, they believe for a while and in time of temptation fall away. {14} And as for what fell among the thorns, they are those who hear, but as they go on their way **they are choked by the cares and riches and pleasures of life,** and their fruit does not mature. {15} And as for that in the good soil, **they are those who, hearing the word, hold it fast in an honest and good heart, and bring forth fruit with patience.**" (Lk. 8:4-15)

What is the Gospel?
[124-129, 571]

"For God so loved the world that he gave his only Son, that whoever believes in him should not perish but have eternal life." (Jn. 3:16)"...the power of God for salvation to every one who has faith." (Rm. 1:16)"Now I recall to your minds, the gospel that I preached to you, through which also you are being saved, that Christ died for our sins according to the scriptures, and that he was buried, and that he rose again the third day, according to the scriptures, and that he appeared to Cephas. Then he was seen by more than five hundred at one time, last of all he was seen also by me." (1 Cor. 15:1-6)" And there is salvation in no one else, for there is no other name under heaven given among men by which we must be saved." (Acts 4:12)

Why does God allow evil?
[309-324]

1. (**To test us**) We can't know the full answer because then there would be no need for faith or trust in God. God gives us examples of how He has drawn good out of evil in the past, in other situations, that we may trust Him in the future, in our situation. *"Those who trust in him shall understand truth." (Wis. 3:9) "The Lord gave and the Lord has taken away; blessed be the name of the Lord!" (Job. 1:21) "We accept good things from God; and should we not accept evil?" (Job. 2:10)* Also read: Job. 1, 2, 38-42, 1 Pt. 4:12-18.

2. (**To preserve free will**) A man on a mountain can see ahead of others on the ground, and know any dangers they are walking to, but his knowledge does not cause them. So too, God's knowledge of who is saved or lost does not cause this to happen. Knowing is not the same as causing, we are truly free. *"When God, in the beginning, created man, he made him subject to his own free choice. If you choose you can keep the commandments; ...Before man are life and death, whichever he chooses shall be given him." (Sir. 15:14-17) "Do not be deceived, God is not mocked. For what a man sows, that he will also reap." (Gal. 6:7, 8)*

3. **(To draw good out of evil)** *"You intended evil against me, but God intended it for good, to do as he has done today, namely, to save the lives of many people."* (Gen. 50:20) *"As I live, says the Lord God, I swear I take no pleasure in the death of the wicked man, but rather in the wicked man's conversion, that he may live."* (Ezek. 33:11) *"The Son of Man came to seek and to save what was lost."* (Lk. 19:10) *"I came to call sinners, not the just."* (Mk. 2:17) *God makes sinners into saints.*

4. **(Through the great evil of the crucifixion—the murder of the sinless Son of God—God brought about the great good of redemption: salvation for the world)** *"Did not the Christ have to suffer these things before entering into his glory?"* (Lk. 24:26) Do not we have to suffer before sharing in his glory? *"Through his suffering, my servant shall justify many...he shall take away the sins of many, and win pardon for their offenses."* (Is. 53:11, 12)

5. **(To conquer evil)** *"Overcome evil with good."* (Rom. 12:21)

6. **(To give us a means to a greater reward and enable us to unite our suffering to Christ as penance for sins)** *"He who overcomes, I will permit him to sit with me upon my throne; as I also have overcome and have sat with my Father on his throne."* (Rev. 3:21, Job. 42:10, 12.) *"I make up in my body what is lacking to the sufferings of Christ, for the sake of his body the church."* (Col. 1:24) By our sufferings we become like Christ, and when we unite our sufferings to His, we help join in the atonement for sin for ourselves and others. If you knew your sacrifices and sufferings could help your soul and others get to heaven, when they were united to Christ's, would it be easier to suffer knowing it had meaning? Christ has called us to be like him even in the crucifixion. It won't necessarily be with wood and nails, but it could be with sorrow and pain caused by evil men at whose hands we suffer innocently like Christ. It could be because of illness or misfortune, but if we bear it with faith instead of anger, we can be like the good thief who accepted his crucifixion and received paradise. *"For as the sufferings of Christ abound in us, so also through Christ does our comfort abound."* (2 Cor. 1:5) God also does this to discipline us, *"And have you forgotten the exhortation which addresses you as sons? -- "My son, do not regard lightly the discipline*

of the Lord, nor lose courage when you are punished by him. {6} For the Lord disciplines him whom he loves, and chastises every son whom he receives." {7} It is for discipline that you have to endure. God is treating you as sons; for what son is there whom his father does not discipline? {8} If you are left without discipline, in which all have participated, then you are illegitimate children and not sons." (Heb. 12:5-8) *"For I reckon that the sufferings of the present time are not worthy to be compared with the glory to come that will be revealed in us."* (Rom. 8:18). We unite our sufferings to the sufferings of Christ by our faith and life in Christ. In this way we become little lambs of God who are in union with Christ." *For your sake we are put to death all the day long. We are regarded as sheep for the slaughter."* (Rom. 8:36) People who are innocent victims of horrible acts are like Christ. They who suffer unjustly are like the martyrs in the Church. *"For the time has come for the judgement to begin with the household of God; but if it begin first with us, what will be the end of those who do not believe the gospel of God? And if the just man scarcely will be saved, where will the impious and the sinner appear?"* (1 Pt. 4:17-18)

7. **(Why do we allow evil?)** We may well wonder how we would answer this question if God asked it of us. What would we say if God asked, "Why does man allow evil? "Why did they murder my Son? Why do they murder their own children in the womb by abortion? Why did they reject Christ's teachings when He told them the Truth? Why do they continue to reject His teachings 2000 years after His death?" If we ever tried to challenge God on the problem of evil we would come up on the short end. He is in a much better position than we are to question the evils of this world. He is in a much better position to judge us than we are to judge Him. The crucifix is the ultimate answer to the problem of evil. When we look at a crucifix, we don't see God as a tyrant, we see man as a tyrant; we don't see the injustice of God, but the injustice of man. The next time we get upset over the troubles and pains of life, we should look at a crucifix and ask ourselves: "If God could endure the sufferings we unjustly gave Him when He is not a sinner, then why can't we endure the sufferings He has justly allowed us who are sinners?" He has not asked us to endure anything He Himself did not endure.

Ultimately, sin is the cause of all our problems and prayer is the solution. All evils in this world are caused either by original sin (Gen. 3:16-24) or by our sins.

Divine Revelation
[50-141]

Divine Revelation is the Word of God. It is the truth God reveals to us about Himself and what we need to know to enter heaven. Divine Revelation comes to us through Sacred Tradition and Sacred Scripture. *"Hold fast to the traditions you have received whether by word or our epistle."* (2 Thess. 2:15) *Dei verbum 2: "It pleased God, in His goodness and wisdom, to reveal Himself and to make known the mystery of His will (cf. Eph. 1:9)."*

Sacred Tradition
[75-79]

Tradition is the spoken Word of God passed on from Christ to the Apostles and from the Apostles to the Church (2 Thess. 2:15, 1 Cor. 11:2, 34 Mt. 28:19). It is found in the Creed, Church Council Documents, writings of Popes, Church Fathers, Doctors, Liturgy and the Church's tradition of prayer. (See also:1 Cor. 11:2, Gal.1:8-9, 2 Thess. 2:15, 3:6, 2 Tim. 1:13, 2:2, 3:14.)

Sacred Scripture
[101-141]

Sacred Scripture is the written Word of God, it contains the history of salvation. *"All scripture is inspired by God, and useful for teaching."* (2 Tim. 3:16) God is the primary Author of Sacred Scripture (The Bible).

If you have never read the Bible before, I recommend that you start with Luke, John, and Acts. St. Jerome says: "Ignorance of the Scriptures is ignorance of Christ." (Vat. II, Dei Verbum.VI)

The Nicene Creed:
A Short Summary of God's Revelation
(Catholics say this at every Sunday Mass)
[185-197]

[This is similar to the Apostles Creed with an emphasis on Christ's Divinity, written by the council of Nicea (325 A.D) to fight the Arian Heresy.]

We Believe in one God, the Father, the Almighty, maker of heaven and earth, of all that is seen and unseen. We believe in one Lord, Jesus Christ, the only son of God, eternally begotten of the Father, God from God, Light from Light, true God from true God, begotten, not made, one in Being with the Father. Through him all things were made. For us men and for our salvation he came down from heaven: by the power of the Holy Spirit he was born of the Virgin Mary, and became man. For our sake he was crucified under Pontius Pilate; he suffered, died, and was buried. On the third day he rose again in fulfillment of the Scriptures; he ascended into heaven and is seated at the right hand of the Father. He will come again in glory to judge the living and the dead, and his kingdom will have no end. We believe in the Holy Spirit, the Lord, the giver of life, who proceeds from the Father and the Son. With the Father and the Son he is worshiped and glorified. He has spoken through the prophets. We believe in one holy catholic and apostolic Church. We acknowledge one baptism for the forgiveness of sins. We look for the resurrection of the dead, and the life of the world to come. Amen.

Bible Only Theory
[82]

The Catholic Church rejects the "Bible only" theory because the Bible cannot interpret itself "...*So Philip ran to him, and heard him reading Isaiah the prophet, and asked, "Do you understand what you are reading?" And he said, "How can I, unless some one guides me?"* (Acts 8:27-31, 2 Pt.1:20, 21, 3:15, 16). The fact that many Bible Christians disagree on such important issues as abortion, divorce, and infant baptism, is enough to prove that the Bible cannot stand alone and explain itself; there must be a central authority to interpret it. We believe the Church is authorized by God since scripture calls the Church, "*the pillar and mainstay of the truth*" (1 Tim. 3:15). God guided the Church to decide which books would make up the Bible, as evidenced by the Council of Rome in 382 A.D. God guides this same Church to interpret it. One Christian with a copy of the Bible cannot interpret doctrine for himself which contradicts the Church any more than a citizen with a copy of the Constitution has authority to interpret it for the U.S. without the guidance of the Supreme Court. The "Bible only" theory is not taught by the Bible, is dependent upon the modern technology of the printing press, was never taught by the apostles, and didn't exist until 1500 A.D.

Science, Religion, and Relativism
[159, 2293, 2294]

Evolution is a *theory* of much scientific debate; however, we are allowed to believe God may have created *through* evolution. Science is limited to the physical world and cannot explain or reveal spiritual realities. Science can tell us how things are made, but not who made them or why. Science cannot tell us what is right or wrong, or what we should live for, only Divine Revelation can.

If we were in a bank robbery we wouldn't be likely to question the reality of the robber's bullets based on our "feelings". The same God who made the physical laws made the spiritual. Our "feelings" do not change physical or spiritual realities. Physical and Spiritual truths are consistent and apply the same for all, they are not changed for each individual.

Who is God?
[198-231]

God is our Father (Is. 64:7, Mt. 6:9)
God is our Creator (Gen. 1:1)
God is our Savior (Lk .1:47)
God is Eternal (Ps. 90:2, 4)
God is all Powerful [*Omnipotent*] (Lk. 1:37)
God is all Knowing [*Omniscient*] (1 Sam. 2:3)
God is Present Everywhere *[Omnipresent]* (Ps. 139:7-12)

God is all Good [*Omnibenevolent*] (Ps. 136:1)
God is Just (Ps. 119:37)
God is Merciful and Kind (Lk. 6:36, Jon. 4:2)
God is Holy (Lev. 19:2)
God is One (Mk. 12:29, 32)
God is the Father, Son, and Holy Spirit (Mt. 28:19)

The Holy Trinity
[232-267]

The Holy Trinity is a mystery, we can have only a partial understanding of it. God possesses one divine nature in three Divine Persons. A nature is what something or someone is. A person is who someone is. God is one Divine Nature, but He is Three Divine Persons: God the Father, God the Son, and God the Holy Spirit (Mt. 28:19, Gen. 3:22) A common analogy is water, which is one substance, but has three forms: gas (clouds), liquid (water) and solid (ice).

Jesus Christ
[422-682]

Jesus Christ is the Eternal Son of God, the Second Divine Person of the Holy Trinity, Who became man for our salvation. His death paid our debt for sin, and merited Eternal life for us. Dying He destroyed our death, rising He restored our Life. Jesus is both God and Man, both "Son of God" and "Son of Man". Scripture teaches that Christ is Divine: (Col. 2:9, Jn. 1:1, 5:18, 10:30, 20:28, Is. 9:5, 6, Mt. 1:23)

He is "the Son of God" (Mt. 4:3), *"the Savior of the world"* (Jn. 4:42) and, *"The lamb of God who takes away the sin of the world."* (Jn. 1:29) Of Himself He says:

I am the Alpha and the Omega, the beginning and the end. (Rev. 21:6)
I am the resurrection and the Life; he who believes in me, even if he
die, shall live. (Jn. 11:25)
I am the Way, and the Truth, and the Life. No one comes to the
Father but through me. (Jn. 14:6)
I am the bread of Life. (Jn. 6:35)
I am the light of the world. (Jn. 8:12)
I am the door. (Jn. 10:7)

I am the good shepherd. (Jn. 10:11)
I am the true vine. (Jn. 15:1)
Before Abraham came to be- I AM. (Jn. 8:58, cf. Ex. 3:14)

God the Holy Spirit
[683-747]

The Holy Spirit is the Divine Third Person of the Holy Trinity. The scriptures say:

The Holy Spirit is God (Jn. 4:24, Acts 5:3, 4, Jn. 4:24, Gen 6:3).
The Holy Spirit is the Spirit of truth (Jn. 14:17)
The Holy Spirit is the Spirit of God (Mt. 3:16, Gen. 1:2)
The Holy Spirit is the Spirit of life (Rom. 8:2\Rev. 11:11)
The Holy Spirit dwells within the servants of God
　　(Ezek. 36:27\1 Cor. 6:17\1 Cor. 3:16)
The Holy Spirit makes our bodies His Temple (1 Cor. 6:19,20)
The Holy Spirit is the Spirit of Love (2 Tim. 1:7\1Jn. 4:16),
The Spirit of Grace (Zech. 12:10),
The Spirit of Holiness (2 Thess. 2:13),
The Spirit of Joy (1 Thess. 1:6\Rom. 14:17)
The Holy Spirit is power from on High (Is. 32:15\Lk. 24:49)
The Holy Spirit helps us under persecution
　　(Mt.. 10:17-20\Mk. 13:11\Lk. 21:14, 15)
The Holy Spirit is given to those who believe in Jesus and keep his
　　commandments(1 Jn. 3:23, 24\1 Jn. 4:13\1 Cor. 12:3\Acts 5:29-32)

The Seven Gifts and Twelve Fruits of the Holy Spirit
[1831,1832]

Seven Gifts:
　　1. Wisdom　2. Understanding　3. Counsel　4. Fortitude
　　5. Knowledge　6. Piety　7. Fear of the Lord (Is. 11:2, 3)

Twelve Fruits:
　　1. Charity　2. Joy.　3. Peace　4. Patience　5. Kindness　6. Goodness
　　7. Long-suffering　8. Humility　9. Fidelity　10. Modesty
　　11. Continence　12. Chastity (Gal. 5:22, 23, 24)

Four Symbols of the Holy Spirit

Dove—Gen. 8:10-12\Mk. 1:10
Fire—Ex. 3:2\Ex. 19:18/Lk. 3:16\Acts 2:3, 4
Water—Gen. 1:2\Jn. 4:14\Jn. 7:37-39\Jn. 3:5
Wind—Jn. 3:8\Acts 2:2\Jn. 20:22\Gen. 2:7

Angels: Messengers of God
[328-354]

Angels are spirits created by God. Man has both flesh and spirit, body and soul, but angels do not have bodies. Angels are:

1. Ministering spirits (Heb. 1:14).
2. Angels can appear to man as having a body (Tobit. 12:19), and are described as having wings (Ex. 25:20, 37:9, Ezek. 10:5).
3. Angels can appear as visible spirits (Lk. 1:11).
4. Angels never die (Lk. 20:36).
5. Angels do not marry (Mt.. 22:30).
6. Angels are stronger than men (2 Pt. 2:11).
7. Angels are messengers (Lk. 1:19).
8. Angels are great in number (Dan.7:10, Rev. 5:11, Mt. 26:53)
9. Angels were created by God (Ex. 20:11, Col.1:16).
10. Angels were created before man and rejoiced at the creation of the world (Job 38:4-7).
11. Angels in heaven rejoice at man's conversion (Lk. 15:10).
12. Angels are our fellow servants of God (Rev. 22:9).

The Nine Choirs of Angels

1. Seraphim (Is. 6:1, 2 or Is. 6:1-7)
2. Cherubim (Gen. 3:24\Ps.80:2, Ezek. 10:4, 5)
3. Thrones (Col. 1:16)
4. Dominations (Col. 1:16)
5. Virtues (Eph. 1:21)
6. Powers (Eph. 3:10)
7. Principalities (Eph. 1:21)

8. Archangels (Jude 9, Tobit. 12:15)
9. Angels (Ps. 8:6)

Guardian Angels
[335, 336]

Everyone has a guardian angel to help protect him from spiritual and physical harm "*It is his angel!*" (Acts 12:15) "*See that you do not despise one of these little ones; for I tell you that in heaven their angels always behold the face of my Father.*" (Mt. 18:10, Gen. 48:16, Ps. 91:11, 12, Ex.23:20, Heb.1:14).

The Devil
[391-395]

The devil was created as a good angel called, "Lucifer", a name which means "Lightbearer". He chose to sin against God (Ezek. 28:12-17, Is. 14:11-15). After this his name was changed to Satan. He led a rebellion against God and some other angels followed him in this. They are called demons. "*Now war arose in heaven, Michael and his angels fighting against the dragon; and the dragon and his angels fought, but they were defeated and there was no longer any place for them in heaven. And the great dragon was thrown down, that ancient serpent, who is called the Devil and Satan, the deceiver of the whole world—he was thrown down to the earth, and his angels were thrown down with him.*" (Rev. 12:7-9) Scripture teaches:

He is Satan. (Rev. 12:7), the Devil (Mt. 4:1)
He is the tempter (Mt.. 4:3), the accuser. (Rev. 12:10)
He is the adversary (1 Pt. 5:8), the enemy. (Mt. 13:39)
He disguises himself as an angel of light. (2 Cor. 11:14)
He is god of this present age. (2 Cor. 4:4)
He is the god of this world. (2 Cor. 4:4, Jn. 14:30, 12:31)
He is the Ancient serpent. (Rev. 12, Gen. 3:1)
He is the evil spirit. (1 Sam. 16:14)
He was a murderer from the beginning. (Jn. 8:44)
He is the angel of the bottomless pit. (Rev. 9:11)

He is the Deceiver of the world. (Rev. 12)
He is the Prince of death. (Heb. 2:14)
He is the ruler of the darkness of this world. (Eph. 6:12)
He is the Father of lies. (Jn. 8:44)

Creation and The Fall of Man
[279-421]

"In the beginning God created the heavens and the earth." (Gen. 1:1). Man is a creature composed of body and soul, and created in the image of God (Gen. 1:26\2:7). The fall of man is his fall from grace into sin. Adam and Eve were the first man and woman created by God. They were created in grace or friendship with God. They were tempted by the devil to disobey God (Gen. 3) and committed the first (original) sin. They lost their friendship with God, and were driven out of the Garden of Eden into a world of suffering and death — for them and their descendants (Ps. 51:7, Rom. 5:12).

Grace
[1996-2005]

Grace is a necessary supernatural gift of God which confers new life onto the soul — God's own Divine life. Grace is a free gift of God which is based on Christ's work on the cross. *"For by grace you have been saved through faith; and this is not your own doing, it is the gift of God — not because of works, lest any man should boast."* (Eph. 2:8-10). "Since the initiative belongs to God in the order of grace, **no one can merit the initial grace of forgiveness and justification,** at the beginning of conversion. Moved by the Holy Spirit and by charity, we can then merit for ourselves and for others the graces needed for our sanctification, for the increase of grace and charity, and for the attainment of eternal life." (CCC, 2010). God does reward us for responding to His grace: *"....pray to your Father who is in secret; and your Father who sees in secret will reward you."* (Mt. 6:6, 5:46, Rev. 19:8). We grow in grace through receiving the sacraments, through prayer, reading scripture, and performing acts of charity. We lose grace through sin. The two main types of grace are sanctifying grace and actual grace.

Sanctifying Grace
[2000]

Without sanctifying grace we cannot enter into heaven. It makes us holy and pleasing to God. Being filled with sanctifying grace makes us children of God and gives us a right to heaven. We should have sanctifying grace at all times. *"But we believe that we shall be saved through the grace of the Lord Jesus..."* (Acts 15:11)

Actual Grace
[2000]

Actual graces are special working graces sent to us as we need them to do good works or resist temptation.

Original Sin
[396-409]

Original sin is the sin of our first parents, which deprived us of grace and friendship with God. It has caused us to have a weakened will so that it is harder for us to do good and avoid evil. (Gen. 3, Ps. 51:7) Original sin is called "sin" in an analogical sense, since it is a sin that we have "contracted", but not "committed". It is a condition, not an action. It is not a "personal sin" or "actual sin" which we committed.

Actual Sin
[1849-1851]

Sin is an action against God's will and commandments. *"He who knows how to do the right thing and does not do it commits sin."* (Jam. 4:17) (1 Jn. 3:4). There are different degrees of sin: (Mt. 5:19, Jn. 19:11)

Mortal Sin
[1854-1874]

Mortal sin deprives the soul of sanctifying grace. Those who die with an unrepented mortal sin on their soul cannot enter heaven. "...

I warned you before that those who do such things shall not inherit the kingdom of God." (Gal. 5:21). (See also: 1 Jn. 5:16, 17, Jn. 15:6, Gal. 5:19-21, Heb. 10:26-31). There are three conditions necessary for a mortal sin:

1. **Serious matter**—the thought, word, action or omission must be seriously wrong or believed to be. (Lk. 12:47, 48, Gen. 20:1-8),
2. **Sufficient reflection**—the person must be mindful of the serious wrong (think about it before you do it),
3. **Full consent**—(freely choose to commit the sin).

Venial Sin
[1862, 1863]

Venial sin is a sin which does not involve serious matter, or one in which one of the three conditions for a mortal sin is missing.

Occasion of Sin
[226]

A person, place, or thing which leads us to sin is an occasion of sin. (Mt. 5:29, 30, Pr. 4:14, 15, Sir. 9:3-13)

Nine Ways We Can Share In The Guilt Of Another's Sin
[1868]

We may share in or cause the guilt of another's sin through the following ways:

1. By counsel.
2. By command.
3. By consent.
4. By provocation.
5. By praise or flattery.
6. By concealment.
7. By being a partner in sin.
8. By silence.
9. By defending the ill done.

The Four Sins Crying To Heaven For Vengeance

1. Willful murder (Gen. 4:8-16)

2. Sodomy (Gen. 18:20; 19:12, 13, 24, 25, Rom. 1:18-32)
3. Oppression of the poor (Prov. 14:31)
4. Defrauding laborers of their wages (Jm. 5:4)

The Church: The Body of Christ
[787-796]

The Church is: The Communion of Saints—Apostles' Creed (Heb. 10:25), The Body of Christ (Eph. 1:23, 1 Cor. 12:27), and the Family of God (Eph. 3:15).

The Four Marks of the Church
[813-873]

One—All members believe one faith under the Pope (Eph. 4:4-6, Jn. 17:21).
Holy - Because of its teachings, its sacraments, and its founder, Christ.
Catholic - Universal, the same in doctrine for all people (Mt. 28:19, 20).
Apostolic - it was founded through the Apostles (Eph. 2:20, Rev. 21:14).

The Pope
[552-567]

The word Pope means "Father". The Pope is the Chief Shepherd of the Church, he is the primary teacher and ruler. The Pope is the infallible interpreter of revelation for Catholics. The Pope is only infallible as Chief shepherd of the church when he clearly defines a matter concerning faith or morals. He does not make new revelation, but clarifies the original revelation of Christ and the Apostles. The Pope is not impeccable (incapable of sinning). Belief in infallibility is inescapable; it is not an option. We either believe the Pope, ourselves, or someone else to be the infallible (reliable) guide to scripture. We must trust in someone's interpretation of scripture. Catholics trust the Pope because He was appointed by Christ. *"You are Peter, and upon this rock I will build my church, and the gates of hell will not prevail against it."* (Mt. 16:17-19) *"I have prayed for you that your faith may not fail."* (Lk. 22:31, 32) Christ named him Peter "Cephas", which in Hebrew means "foundation stone". "I will give you the keys to the kingdom of heaven; and whatever you shall bind on earth shall be bound in heaven." (Mt.16:19) The "keys" symbolize authority (Is. 22:15-25, Rev. 1:18). He says to Peter: *"Feed my sheep"*(Jn. 21:15-17) which means "teach my church." He appoints Peter as Chief Shepherd of His church. Christ is the invisible head of the Church, the Pope is the visible head. Scripture shows the first dispute over doctrine was settled by a church council in which Peter played a decisive role as the first Pope (Acts15:7-12). This is the scriptural model for settling disputes over doctrine. Peter is listed first in every list of Apostles (Mt. 10:1-4, Mk. 3:16-19, Lk. 6:12-16, Acts 1:13), first to work a miracle in His name (Acts 3:6-7), and first to preach the gospel (Acts 2:14).

Jesus knew His church would need leadership to function after His Ascension. Jesus established Peter to be the first in a line of successors who would lead the Church in His name after His Ascension. Since Jesus knew it would be centuries until His return it would make no sense for Jesus to provide leadership only for a few years during the life of St. Peter, and then not provide the same authority to His successors after Peter's death.

Jesus even recognized the Authority of the corrupt Pharisees as successors to Moses. *"The scribes and Pharisees sit on Moses' seat; so practice and observe whatever they tell you, but not what they do; for they preach, but do not practice."* Mt. 23:2, 3, Jn. 11:49-52) How much more does he recognize the authority of the successors of the Chair of St. Peter (Feb. 22)! The writings of the early church witness to this:

Around 96 A.D. Pope St. Clement wrote a strong letter to the Church in Corinth to settle a dispute, showing the authority of the Church of Rome, founded on the Apostle Peter, over churches outside Rome. St. Cyprian of Carthage, [251 A.D.] *"...On him [Peter] he builds the Church, and to him he gives the command to feed the sheep [Jn. 21:17], and although he assigns a like power to all the apostles, yet he founded a single chair [cathedra], and he established by his own authority a source and an intrinsic reason for that unity. Indeed, the others were also what Peter was [i.e., apostles], but a primacy is given to Peter, whereby it is made clear that there is but one Church and one chair. So too, all [the apostles] are shepherds, and the flock is shown to be one, fed by all the apostles in single-minded accord. If someone does not hold fast to this unity of Peter, can he imagine that he still holds the faith? If he [should] desert the chair of Peter upon whom the Church was built, can he still be confident that he is in the Church?"* (The Unity of the Catholic Church 4;1st edition [A.D. 251] from www.catholic.com, The Authority of the Pope: Part 1)

St. Irenaeus, [180 A.D.] *"I need only cite the case of that very great, most ancient and universally known church founded and established at Rome by those two most glorious apostles Peter and Paul and draw attention to the tradition which that church has received from the apostles and to the faith it preaches which has come down to our time through the succession of bishops. For in view of the outstanding pre-eminence of this church, there cannot be any disagreement between it and every other church (that is, the faithful in every place)—every church, that is, in which men in every place have at all times preserved the apostolic tradition..."* (*Irenaeus,, "Against Heresies" Book III, 1-3, 1180 A.D. in Official Catholic Teachings: Bible Interpretation*, ed. James J. Megivern Wilmington, N.C.: A Consortium Book from McGrath Pub. Co., 1978, 6, 7.) In the fourth century St. Augustine said, *"Rome has spoken; the case is closed."* When Pope St. Leo the Great gave clear teaching on Christ's divinity at the Council of Chalcedon in 451 A.D., the bishops present said: *"Peter has spoken through Leo!"*

The Blessed Virgin Mary: The New Eve
[494]

Mary is called *"Blessed"* (Lk. 1:42, 48) *"Virgin"* (Mt.1:23), *"the Mother of Jesus"* (Acts 1:14), and the Mother of God. The Bible calls Christ the New Adam." *For as in Adam all die, so in Christ all will be made to live"* (1 Cor.15:22). The early Church Fathers called Mary the New Eve (Gen. 3:15). Death came through Eve, life came through Mary. A fallen angel deceived Eve, a sinless virgin (Gen. 3:4); she disobeyed God and brought death to the world. A good angel gave truth to a sinless *"virgin named Mary"* (Lk. 1:27); she obeyed God and brought life to the world. God uses the same instruments the devil used for our fall as the instruments for our redemption: two sinless sons of God—Adam (Lk. 3:38) and Christ, two sinless virgins—Mary and Eve, two trees—the tree of knowledge and the cross, two angels—Devil and Gabriel.

The Annunciation

In the sixth month the angel Gabriel was sent from God to a city of Galilee named Nazareth, to a virgin betrothed to a man whose name was Joseph, of the house of David; and the virgin's name was Mary. And he came to her and said, *"Hail, full of grace, the Lord is with you!"* Luke 1:26-28

Mary, the Mother of God
[495]

Mary is the Mother of God because she gave birth to Jesus who is both God and man. (Lk. 1:43, Jn. 20:28) Mary is our spiritual mother. (Jn. 19:25-27, Rev. 12: 1, 17, Gen. 3:20)

Immaculate Conception
[491-492]

The Immaculate Conception means that Mary was conceived without sin. This was to prepare her for a special role as the Mother of God, when she would conceive by the Holy Spirit (Lk. 1:26-38\Mt. 1:18, 19, 20). God chose to apply the anticipated merits of Jesus Christ to her soul at the moment of her conception and preserve her from original sin. In the beginning God created a sinless man and woman who fell, in the new beginning of redemption God would have another sinless man and woman *"full of grace"* (Lk. 1:28, Jn. 1:14) who would never fall.

Mary's Perpetual Virginity
[496-510]

Mary is called a Perpetual Virgin because she was a virgin, before, during, and after the birth of Christ. (Lk. 1:34, Is. 7:14) Note that the Greek term used for the "brothers" (Mk. 3:31) of Jesus means cousin or brother.

Mary's Assumption into Heaven
[966, 974]

Mary was assumed, body and soul, into heaven. Mary deserved the honor of being assumed into heaven because she was free of sin and its consequences. Elijah and Enoch were assumed into heaven (Gen. 5:24, 2 Kings 2, Heb. 11:5, 6), and Mary had an even higher role in the plan of salvation.

The Birth of Christ

And she gave birth to her first-born son and wrapped him in swaddling cloths, and laid him in a manger, because there was no place for them in the inn. Luke 2:7

Jesus works His first Miracle through Mary's Intercession

When the wine failed, the mother of Jesus said to him, *"They have no wine."*... This, the first of his signs, Jesus did at Cana in Galilee, and manifested his glory; and his disciples believed in him. John 2:3, 11

The Intercession of Mary
[969-975]

Catholics worship only God, but they honor Mary as their spiritual Mother, *"And a great portent appeared in heaven, a woman clothed with the sun, with the moon under her feet, and on her head a crown of twelve stars [Mary, Queen of Heaven]...She brought forth a male child [Jesus], one who is to rule all the nations...Then the dragon [the devil] was angry with the woman, and went off to make war on the rest of her offspring [members of the Church, the body of Christ], on those who keep the commandments of God and bear testimony to Jesus."* (Rev.12:1-17, Jn. 19:26, 27). Mary is a creature, not the creator. However, Mary is the Mother of God (Lk. 1:43, Jn. 20:28). She is our Mother, and the Queen of Heaven. Lk. 1:48: *"For Behold, henceforth all generations will call me blessed."* We are commanded by God to *"Honor your Father and Mother"*(Ex. 20:12), thus the honor we give to Mary our Spiritual Mother in no way subtracts from the worship we give to God any more than honoring our earthly mother does. In fact, it conforms to God's holy will, and we who are sons of God honor her whom the Son of God honored.

Christ is our only mediator (1 Tim. 2:5-6) with the Father, but Mary can intercede (pray for us) with her Son Jesus. Jesus worked His first miracle at her request (Jn. 2:1-12). Just as we can ask other members of the church on earth to pray for us (1 Tim. 2:1, 2 Tim. 1:3, Phil. 4, 22), so, too, we can ask members of the church in heaven to pray for us. (Rev. 5:8, 6:9-11, 7:10-12, 8:2-6, Mt. 22:31, 32). As a builder is honored when someone admires his work, God is honored when we honor Mary. God loves us to honor Mary as a Father is pleased when his daughter is honored. All the honor we give to Mary is reflected back to God since we honor her for what He has done for her, with her, and through her. When we honor her we honor Him.

Statues of Mary and the Saints

Statues of Mary and the Saints are not "idols" (Ex. 20:4) any more than the images of the Cherubim with wings (Ex. 25:20, 37:9) which God commanded to be made for the ark are "idols". In our home, we have pictures of family members whom we love which are displayed for honor, not worship or idolatry. In Church, the house of God, we have pictures and statues of the Saints, members of God's family, whom we love. These we honor; we do not worship them.

The Parallels of Eden and Calvary

The Garden of Eden	The Hill of Calvary
Adam, "Son of God" (Lk. 3:38)	Christ, "New Adam" (1 Cor. 15:22)
Eve (2 Cor. 11:3)	Mary (Lk. 1:27)
Eve: Created without sin	Mary: Conceived without sin
Death by Eve	Life through Mary

Mother of all living (Gen. 3:20)

Mother of all saved (Rev. 12:17)

Temptation by Lucifer, an
evil angel to Eve,
a sinless virgin.

Annunciation from the Good
Angel Gabriel to Mary,
A sinless virgin.

Eve disobeys God.

Mary obeys God.

Tree of Knowledge (Gen. 2:9)

Tree of the Cross (Jn. 19:17)

Man and woman next
to the tree at the
first sin (Gen. 3:6)

Man and woman next to the cross
at the atonement for sin (Jn. 19:26)

Forbidden to eat
from the tree of life
(Gen. 3:22)

Christ gives us the Eucharist, the
Fruit from the new tree of life—the
cross. (Mt. 26:26-29)

Punishment for the
Sin of Adam causes
the ground to bring
forth thorns. (Gen. 3:18)

Bearing our punishment for sin,
Christ is crowned with a crown
of thorns. (Mt. 27:29)

Adam earned his earthly
bread by the sweat of
his brow (Gen. 3:19)
in his labors on
The cursed ground (Gen. 3:17)

Christ earned for us the heavenly
Bread (Jn. 6:51) of the Eucharist
In the work of his passion,
Starting with sweating blood
On the ground. (Lk. 22:44)

An angel is placed in
the Garden to keep
man out. (Gen. 3:24)

An angel is placed in the Garden
to strengthen Christ. (Lk. 22:43)

The Side of Adam
opened by God gives
birth to his bride Eve
during sleep. (Gen. 2:21)

The Side of Christ, pierced by a
lance gives birth to
His bride the Church
during sleep of death. (Jn. 19:34)

Exiled from Paradise. (Gen. 3:23)	Opened the gates of Paradise (Lk. 23:43)
Driven from Garden (Gen. 3:23)	Entered the Garden (Jn. 18:1)
Clothed after sin. (Gen. 3:7, 21)	Stripped at crucifixion. (Mk. 15:24)
Cain slays Abel (Gen.4:8)	The Good Thief (St. Dysmus) rebukes the Bad Thief. (Lk. 23:39-43)
Adam and Eve gave in to evil and brought death to all their descendants.	Christ and Mary overcame evil and brought life to all their spiritual descendants.
God breathed into Adam the breath of life and he became alive. (Gen. 2:7)	Christ breathed on the Apostles the Holy Spirit and the power to forgive sins, and through his priests breathed spiritual life into dead souls. (Jn. 20:22, 23)

Apparitions of Mary

The Church allows, not requires, us to believe that Mary has appeared to us on earth after her Assumption to Heaven. There are several approved apparitions (appearances) of Mary such as Guadalupe, Lourdes, and Fatima. Scripture says that other saints can appear to people on earth (Mt. 17:3, Mt. 27:52, 53). If lesser saints can appear to people on earth, how much more can Mary, the Mother of God?

The Last Judgement
[1038-1041]

At death, each soul receives his own individual judgement by God. At the end of the world, Christ will return to the earth and judge it (Mt. 25, Wis.1-5). He will restate the individual judgement we received at death in front of the whole world. At this time all the dead will rise (1 Cor. 15, Dan. 12:2, 3). *"And I saw a great white throne and the one who sat upon it; from his face the earth and heaven fled away, and there was found no place for them. And I saw the dead, the great and the small, standing before the throne, and scrolls were opened. And another scroll was opened, which is the book of life; and the dead were judged out of those things that were written in the scrolls, according to their works... And if anyone was not found written in the book of life, he was cast into the pool of fire."* (Rev. 20:11-13)

Heaven
[1023-1029]

Heaven is a place of reward and eternal happiness for those who do God's will on earth and die in a state of grace. *"Well done, good and faithful servant; because you have been faithful over a few things, I will set you over many; enter into the joy of your master."* (Mt. 25:21) *"And he said to Jesus, 'Lord, remember me when you come into your kingdom.' And Jesus said to him, 'This day you shall be with me in paradise.'"* (Lk. 23:42, 43) (Rev. 21:3, 4, 1 Cor. 2:9) There are different degrees of reward in heaven because each receives according to his works (Mk. 4:20, 10:35-40, Lk. 19:17, 19, 1 Cor. 3:8, 15:41, 42, 2 Cor. 9:6-8, Mt. 16:27).

Hell
[1033-1037]

Hell is a place of eternal punishment for those who die in a state of mortal sin and consequently have rejected God's life, truth, and love. The two main punishments of hell are the "pain of loss" (eternal loss of friendship with God) and the "pain of sense" (eternal torment of the senses). *"Depart from me, accursed ones, into the everlasting fire prepared for the devil and his angels."* (Mt. 25:41) (Mk. 9:42-47, Lk. 16:19-31, Mt. 10:28)

Why does God Allow Hell to Exist?

Some say: "How can hell be eternal and God still be just?" We need to look at the injustice that would result if there were no hell. God cannot give the good and the evil the same reward. He cannot take away free will, and force men to love Him. He cannot force forgiveness on them if they do not admit their guilt, and ask for forgiveness. He cannot allow them to continue to sin against God and neighbor forever without punishment. Hell is a way to preserve the free will of man to reject God, and to allow God to keep justice in the universe by punishing them for their evil choice. We must remember that the evil receive their reward in this life, but the good receive it in the next. *"But Abraham said, 'Son, remember that you in your lifetime received your good things, and Lazarus in like manner evil things; but now he is comforted here, and you are in anguish."* (Lk. 16:25)

See: Lk. 6:19-31, Ps. 17:14, Mt. 6:2, 5, Ps. 73, 37, and 49. Reincarnation is a false belief which contradicts the teachings of Christ regarding judgement and the afterlife (Heb. 9:27).

Purgatory
[1030-1032]
Purgatory is a temporary place where souls go to complete purification which they did not complete on earth. *"It is therefore a holy and wholesome thought to pray for the dead, that they may be loosed from their sins."* (2 Mac. 12:46) (1 Cor. 3:11-15, Mt. 5:23-26)

Part II
The Seven Sacraments
[1210-1666]

"Do this in memory of me." (1 Cor. 11:24)

A sacrament is an outward sign instituted by Christ to give us grace. The sacraments are entrusted to the Church and given as a means by which divine life is dispensed to us. They give graces and bear fruit when we receive them with the proper disposition. Each sacrament has both form and matter. Form constitutes the words used in the administration of the sacrament; matter involves the pouring of water for baptism, bread and wine for mass, anointing with oil for confirmation and the anointing of the sick, contrition for confession, laying on of hands for ordination, and mutual consent for a couple choosing marriage.

1. Baptism: [1213-1284] *"Go therefore and make disciples of all nations, baptizing them in the name of the Father, and of the Son and of the Holy Spirit, teaching them to observe all that I have commanded you..."* (Mt. 28:19,) *"...unless a man be born again of water and the Holy Spirit, he cannot enter into the kingdom of God."* Jn. 3:5 *"I will sprinkle clean water upon you, and you shall be clean from all your uncleannesses...A new heart I will give you and...I will put my spirit within you."* (Ezek. 36:25-27). *"...be baptized and wash away your sins."* Acts 22:16. The sacrament of Baptism is the first sacrament we receive. It is necessary to receive it before receiving the other sacraments. Baptism forgives original sin, actual sin, and infuses sanctifying grace within the soul (Ezek. 36:25, 26, Acts 2:38, 22:16, 1 Cor. 6:11, Gal. 3:26, 27).

"Baptism, which corresponds to this, now saves you." (1 Pt. 3:21)

It applies the merits of Christ's death on the cross to our soul, and cleanses us from sin. It makes us children of God, brothers of Christ, and temples of the Holy Spirit. It can be received only once and leaves an eternal mark upon the face of the soul. In an emergency, when death is imminent and a priest cannot be reached, anyone can baptize by pouring plain water on the forehead while saying: "I baptize you in the name of the Father, and of the Son, and of the Holy Spirit."

2. **Confirmation:** [1285-1321] (*"Then they laid their hands on them, and they received the Holy spirit."* Acts: 8:14-17, 19:5, 6, Tim. 3:4-8) Along with Baptism and the Holy Eucharist, Confirmation is part of the triad of Christian initiation. Confirmation increases and deepens the graces received at baptism. It unites us more firmly to Christ and it increases the gifts of the Holy Spirit within us. It imparts a special strength to witness, spread, and defend the faith. It can be received only once and leaves an eternal mark upon the face of the soul. ...In the Latin rite, "the sacrament of Confirmation is conferred through the anointing with chrism on the forehead, which is done by the laying on of the hand, and through the words: 'Be sealed with the Gift of the Holy Sprit'" (Catechism of the Catholic Church 1300.) *"...he has put his seal upon us and given us his Spirit in our hearts as a guarantee."* (2 Cor. 1:22) *"...believed in him, were sealed with the promised Holy Spirit."* (Eph. 1:13) *"And do not grieve the Holy spirit of God, in whom you were sealed for the day of redemption."* (Eph. 4:30)

3. **Holy Eucharist:** [1322-1419] (Jn. 6:25-71, Mt. 26:26-28, 1 Cor. 11:23-26, Lk. 24:30, 31) The Holy Eucharist is also called "communion" and the "Blessed Sacrament". The Holy Eucharist is "the source and summit of the Christian life." (LG11) It is not a symbol of Christ, but is the Real Body, Blood, Soul, and Divinity of Jesus Christ. During the miracle of the Mass, the priest consecrates (changes) the bread and wine into the Body and Blood of Christ at the words of institution, taken from scripture, which are: *"This is my Body; this is my Blood."* (1 Cor. 11:24, 25).

The same God who worked the miracle of creation when he said, *"Let there be light"*, worked the miracle of the consecration when He said, *"This is my body"*, and it was! Today the priest acts in the person of Christ. Visibly you see Christ's sinful human priests, but invisibly it is Christ Himself who works the miracle of the consecration. The voice of His human priest says the words of consecration, *"this is my body..."* and the power of Christ, the invisible Priest, changes the substance of ordinary bread into *"The living bread come down from heaven."* (Jn. 6:51). "...by the consecration of the bread and wine there takes place a change of the whole substance of the bread into the substance of the body of Christ our Lord and of the whole substance of the wine into the substance of his blood. This change...called *transubstantiation."* (CCC 1376) The appearance and taste of bread and wine remain, but the substance is changed. He who said it then, at the Last Supper, says it now at every mass when He becomes one with the priest and works this miracle conforming to His command: *"Do this in memory of me" (*1 Cor. 11:24).

St. Francis of Assisi said, "Let everyone be struck with fear, the whole world tremble, and the heavens exult when Christ, the Son of the living God, is present on the altar in the hands of a priest!...The Lord of the universe, God and the Son of God, so humbles Himself that He hides Himself for our salvation under an ordinary piece of bread!" (Fr. Benedict J. Groeschel,C.F.R., Praying in the Presence of Our Lord, Our Sunday Visitor Inc. 1999, p. 19) Even at His birth He taught us about the real presence. Christ was born in a manger (a feed box) in Bethlehem (which means "House of bread").

We receive the whole Christ under each species (bread or wine) so, we do not **need** to receive both. If we have committed a mortal sin, we must go to confession before receiving communion. Otherwise, instead of bringing grace to the soul, communion brings the sin of sacrilege. First Holy Communion is part of the initiation into the Catholic Faith. It would be unjust to have two standards of preparation for the Eucharist, to allow a visitor to receive when Catholics are required to strict preparation and beliefs. *"Whoever, therefore, eats the bread or drinks the cup of the Lord in an unworthy manner will be guilty of profaning the body and blood of the Lord. Let a man examine himself, and so eat of the bread and drink of the cup. For any one who eats and drinks without discerning the body eats and drinks judgement*

The Last Supper: The First Mass

"I am the living bread which came down from heaven; if any one eats of this bread, he will live for ever; and the bread which I shall give for the life of the world is my flesh." (John 6:5)

upon himself. That is why many of you are weak and ill, and some have died." (1 Cor. 11:27-30)

To receive communion, one must come forward with his or her hands folded in prayer. When you come before the priest, he will say: "The Body of Christ": showing your belief, you respond, "Amen" (which means "I believe"). GIRM 161: *The communicant replies, Amen, and receives the Sacrament either on the tongue, or, where this is allowed and if the communicant so chooses, in the hand. As soon as the communicant receives the host, he or she consumes it entirely."*

The Four Primary Aspects of the Mass:

1. **New Covenant Meal:** For centuries the passover meal foreshadowed the sacrifice of the Mass, the true Paschal Banquet. At the Last Supper, (the first mass), Christ raised the Passover to its full meaning. At the Passover meal, the unleavened bread and the flesh of the lamb, were a symbol of the body of Christ. *"...every house in which they partake of the lamb. That same night they shall eat its roasted flesh with unleavened bread and bitter herbs."* (Ex. 12:7, 8, 1 Cor. 5:7).

    The bread which was a symbol of Christ for centuries became reality at the last supper. Christ said: *"I am the living bread that has come down from heaven. If anyone eat of this bread he shall live forever; and the bread that I will give is my flesh for the life of the world...he who eats my flesh and drinks my blood has eternal life and I will raise him up at the last day. For my flesh is food indeed, and my blood is drink indeed. He who eats my flesh and drinks my blood abides in me, and I in him."* (Jn. 6:48-56) In holy communion we unite the body, blood, soul, and divinity of Christ with our body, blood, soul, and humanity.

    "Now the day of the Unleavened Bread came, on which the passover had to be sacrificed..And when the hour had come, he reclined at table, and the twelve apostles with him. And he said to them, "I have greatly desired to <u>eat</u> this passover with you before I suffer.." (Lk. 22:7, 14-16) *"The days are coming, says the Lord, when I will make a **new covenant** with the house of Israel and the house of Judah. It will not be like the covenant I made with their fathers the day I took them by the hand to lead them forth from the land of Egypt; for they broke my covenant and I had to show myself their master, says the Lord...I will forgive their evildoing and remember their sin no more."* (Jer. 31:31-34) *"This cup is the **new covenant in my blood**"* (Lk. 22:20)

2. **Memorial:** *"This day shall be a **memorial** feast for you, which all your generations shall celebrate with pilgrimage to the Lord as a **perpetual** institution"* (Ex. 12:14) *"Do this in **remembrance** of me"* (1 Cor. 11:25).

3. **Sacrifice:** "The Eucharist is thus a sacrifice because it re-presents

(makes present) the sacrifice of the cross" (CCC1366)

The mass is the sacrifice of Christ at Calvary offered in an unbloody manner (Heb. 13:10). *"For Christ our Passover has been sacrificed."* (1 Cor. 5:7) *"...the precious blood of Christ, like that of a lamb without blemish or spot."* (1 Pt. 1:18-21). *"The lamb must be a year old male and without blemish...then, with the whole assembly of Israel present, it shall be slaughtered during the evening twilight. They shall take some of its blood and apply it to the two doorposts [symbol of the cross] and the lintel of every house in which they partake of the lamb."* (Ex. 12:5-7) Christ's words are sacrificial terms. "Given up" and "shed", signify the sacrifice (Lk. 22:19, 1 Cor. 11:24). *"my blood, which shall be <u>shed</u> for you."* (Lk. 22:20) *For as often as you shall eat this bread and drink the cup, you **proclaim the death of the Lord** until he comes."* (1 Cor. 11:26) St. Justin Martyr (155 A.D.) wrote that the mass was prophesied in the Old Testament, *"From the rising of the sun to its setting my name is great among the nations, and **every-where they bring sacrifice** to my name, and a **pure offering**; for great is my name among the nations, says the Lord of hosts.* (Mal. 1:11) Abraham went to sacrifice Isaac, his *"only son.. on the third day...on the altar."* (Gen. 22:4, 9) as a foreshadowing of God the Father offering his Son on the cross and the altar at mass. Compare: (Gen. 22:7, 8 and Jn. 1:29, Gen. 22:2, and Jn. 3:16, Gen. 22:6 and Jn. 19:17, 18, Gen. 22:13 and Mt. 27:27, 29) We are called to make sacrifices in life to show our love of God (Lk. 9:23, 1 Cor. 1:18).

4. **Propitiation:** The sacrifice of the Mass appeases the justice of God for our sins. "The Sacrifice of Christ and the sacrifice of the Eucharist are one single sacrifice: 'The victim is one and the same: the same now offers through the ministry of priests, who then offered himself on the cross; only the manner of offering is different.' And since in this divine sacrifice which is celebrated in the Mass, the same Christ who offered himself once in a bloody manner on the altar of the cross is contained and offered in an unbloody manner...this sacrifice is truly propitiatory." (CCC1367)

The destruction of the firstborn of Egypt was a foreshadowing of the Last Judgement. Then, God will finally strike down the evil men of this world and deliver his people from the sufferings and persecutions of this world. Through union with Christ we will exit (*Exodus*) from the slavery of sin. The Israelites who had the blood of the lamb on their doorposts and who ate of the flesh of the lamb were spared the judgement of God. *"For on this same night I will go through Egypt, striking down every first-born of the land, both man and beast, and executing judgement on all the gods of Egypt- I the Lord! But the blood will mark the houses where you are. Seeing the blood, I will pass over you..."* (Ex. 12:12, 13) In the same way will those Catholics who worthily eat of the flesh of the lamb of God, the Eucharist, be spared the judgement of God. God's judgement will **pass over** us because of our union with His son.

Eucharistic Adoration and Benediction
"Could you not watch one hour with me?" (Mt. 26:40)

A Holy Hour is an hour of Eucharistic Adoration, which is a ritual of adoring the Blessed Sacrament outside of mass. In this ceremony, the consecrated host is placed in a special container called a **Monstrance** which enables the people to see the host through a clear glass at its center. **Benediction** is when the priest or deacon takes the Monstrance and makes the sign of the cross over the people, assisting Jesus in the Eucharist, to bless (**Benediction**) the people.

I believe the degree of grace and fulfillment we get at mass and communion is directly related to how much faith we have in the Real Presence of Christ in the Eucharist. Eucharistic Adoration is a preeminent way to increase our faith in the Eucharist. *"The worship of the Eucharist outside of the Mass is of inestimable value for the life of the church....It is the responsibility of Pastors to encourage, also by their personal witness, the practice of Eucharistic adoration.... It is pleasant to spend time with him, to lie close to his breast like the Beloved Disciple (cf. Jn. 13:25) and to feel the infinite love present in his heart.... How can we not feel a renewed need to spend time in spiritual converse, in silent adoration, in heartfelt love before Christ present in the Most Holy Sacrament? St. Alphonsus Liguori... wrote: 'Of all the devotions, that of adoring Jesus in the Blessed Sacrament is the greatest after the sacraments, the one dearest to God and the one most helpful to us."* (Pope John Paul II, Ecclesia de Eucharistia, n. 25).

The Five Liturgical Seasons:
[1163-1173]

1. **Advent:** Signifying the arrival, this begins the Liturgical year by preparing us for the birth of Our Lord at Christmas.
2. **Christmas Season**: Celebration of the Birth of our Lord up to his baptism.
3. **Lent**: A penitential season from Ash Wednesday to Holy Thursday. The last week is Holy Week which celebrates the Passion and death of our Lord. The Triduum begins Holy Thursday, includes Good Friday, and Easter.
4. **Easter Season**: Celebrates from the Resurrection on Easter to Pentecost.
5. **Ordinary Time**: time which does not fall within Advent, Lent, Christmas, or Easter.

Vestments

Vestments are special clothing worn by the Priest to symbolize the unique and supernatural mystery of the mass. In the Old Testament priests wore vestments to symbolize their unique role in ministering for God. ("*...make holy garments for glory and for beauty.*" Ex. 28:1-4, 40, 29:29, Lev. 8:7-9, 16:4, Ps.132:9, Zec. 3:3-5, Ezk. 42:13-14) They also symbolize the clothes of Christ during His passion (Mt. 26:28, Mk. 15:17, Lk. 23:11, Jn. 19:23, 24, Gen. 37:23, 31-34, Rev. 1:13, 19:13). The colors of the vestments reflect different meanings.

The Seven Liturgical Colors:

1. **Green.** For Ordinary Time, a symbol of hope, growth, and life.
2. **White.** For Joyful celebrations of Our Lord and Our Lady. It's a symbol of the resurrection (for funerals), of purity, innocence, virginity, and joy (for Weddings, Baptisms).
3. **Red.** For the Passion of Christ, Pentecost, and the feasts of martyrs. A symbol of sacrifice, of the precious blood, charity, and the fire of the Holy Spirit.

4. **Purple.** A Penitential and sorrowful color for Advent and Lent.
5. **Black.** For funerals, a symbol of death and mourning.
6. **Rose.** For Gaudete Sunday (third Sunday of Advent), and Laetare Sunday (fourth Sunday of Lent). A symbol of subdued joy, relieved repentance.
7. **Gold.** A Festive Color, for Joyful and Glorious celebrations, such as Christ the King. It is a symbol of victory.

Rules for Communion Fast and for the Lenten Fast
[1387]
"When you fast...your Father who sees in secret will reward you."
(Mt. 6:16-18) We are to fast, not eat or drink anything except water, one hour before receiving Holy Communion.

During Lent, Ash Wednesday and Good Friday are days of abstinence and also days of fast. All the Fridays of Lent are days of abstinence. The law of abstinence binds all Catholics over 14 years of age. No meat is to be eaten on days of abstinence. The law of fasting binds all Catholics from their 18th year until the beginning of their 60th year. Only one full meal and two lighter meals are allowed on days of fast. (Canon 1252) Fasting is one of the **Three Eminent Good Works:**
1. **Prayer** (Mt. 6:5-15)
2. **Alms** (Mt. 6:1-4, Gen. 14:20, Lk. 12:33, 21:1-3)
3. **Fasting** (Mt. 6:16-18, 4:2, 9:15, Mk. 9:29)

A Scriptural Guide to the Mass

I The Introductory Rites

1. Introductory Rites
   Sign of Cross (Mt. 28:19) Amen (1 Chr. 13:36) Greeting (2 Cor. 13:13, Ruth 2:4)
2. Penitential Rite A.Confiteor (Jas. 5:16, 1 Jn. 1:9) B. Kyrie (Lk. 18:13, 1 Tim. 1:2, Tb. 8:4)
3. Gloria (Lk. 2:14)
4. Opening Prayer

II Liturgy of the Word

5. 1st Reading (Mostly Old Testament)
6. Responsorial Psalm (One of the 150 Psalms of the Old Testament)
7. Second Reading (All of the New Testament except Gospels)
8. Gospel (Matthew, Mark, Luke, John)
9. Homily (Explanation of how to live the Gospel)
10. Profession of Faith (The Creed is a communal profession of Faith in Jesus Christ, His Gospel and His Catholic Church)
11. General Intercessions (Prayer of the Faithful) (Rev. 8:3-4)

III The Liturgy of the Eucharist

12. Offertory (Preparation of the Gifts) (Jn. 6:35, Ps. 50:23, 68:36)
13. Preface (Is. 6:3, Mk. 12:9-10)
14. Eucharistic Prayer I, II, III, and IV, plus those for children and for reconciliation. (Consecration of Bread and Wine into the Body and Blood of Christ) (Gen. 14:18, Ex. 12, 1 Cor. 5:7, Mal. 1:11, Mt. 26:26-28, Jn. 6:25-71, 1 Cor. 11:23-26, Lk. 24:30, 31, Acts 2:42)
15. Memorial Acclamation (1 Cor. 15:3-5)
16. Lord's Prayer (Mt. 6:9-13)
17. Sign of Peace (Jn. 14:27, 20:19, Mt. 5:23, 24)
18. Lamb of God (Breaking of the Bread) (Jn. 1:29, Pt. 1:18-21, Mt. 8:8)
19. Communion (People receive the Eucharist) (Rev. 19:9)
20. Closing Prayer

IV The Concluding Rites

21. Final Blessing and Dismissal (Lk. 7:50, 24:51, 2 Cor. 9:15)

4. **Penance:** [1422-1498] This sacrament is also called Confession, or Reconciliation. (Prv. 28:13, Matt. 9:6-8) Christ gave the power to forgive sins in His name to the Apostles, and they passed this power on to their successors, the Bishops and Priests. Confession forgives sins committed after baptism. The priest is bound under pain of mortal sin not to reveal anything he has heard in confession. This is called **the seal of the confessional.** A priest would go to jail or die before he would reveal sins that someone confessed to him.

It is essential for the person confessing (the penitent) to be contrite. Contrition is a heartfelt sorrow and repugnance for the sin committed, along with the intention of sinning no more (see Psalm 51). **Imperfect contrition** is sorrow for sin because the sins are hateful in themselves or because the person fears going to hell. Imperfect contrition is necessary for a good confession. **Perfect contrition** is sorrow for sin because sin offends God Whom we love above all things. A person who has committed a mortal sin can regain the state of grace before confession by making a perfect act of contrition with the definite intention of going to confession. However, since it is difficult to know if we have perfect contrition, it is the Church's rule to confess all mortal sins and receive absolution before receiving Holy Communion. To help us understand the great mercy and love of God, we should read Luke 15 and Ezekiel 33. *"As I live, says the Lord God, I have no pleasure in the death of the wicked, but that the wicked turn from his way and live...If he turns from his sin and does what is lawful and right...he shall surely live, he shall not die."* (Ezek. 33:11, 14, 15).

How to go to Confession:

1. Prepare for confession by an examination of conscience followed by contrition. As preparation, the penitent may read from passages on God's mercy such as: Ezek. 33, Lk. 15, Jn. 8:1-11.
2. Make the Sign of the cross. The priest may read a text of holy Scripture.
3. State how long since your last confession.
4. You must confess all mortal sins you can remember according to kind (type, such as adultery or theft) and number (amount, such as once, few, many). It is a sin to deliberately conceal any mortal sins, it is lying to God's representative and this would invalidate the confession (Acts 5:5). However, don't worry about sins you can't remember.
5. The priest tells you what your penance is (i.e., prayers etc.) and may give some spiritual guidance.
6. Pray an act of contrition. [This shows a firm purpose of amendment, that is, one intends to try not to sin again.]
7. Receive absolution. [Priest says: "I absolve you from your sins in the

name of the Father, and of the Son, and of the Holy Spirit." Penitent responds, "Amen."]

8. Proclamation of Praise of God and Dismissal Priest: "Give thanks to the Lord, for He is good." Penitent: "His mercy endures forever." Priest: "The Lord has freed you from your sins, go in peace."
9. Leave the confessional, and go do your penance. (2 Sam. 12:13, 114 1 Chr. 212:8-13, 1 Pt. 4:8, Jm. 5:20)

If you forget how to go to confession simply tell the priest and he will help you.

Why should I confess to a Priest?

Christ Himself gave the power to forgive sins in His name to the Apostles and their successors. "As the Father has sent me, even so I send you." And when he had said this, he breathed on them, and said to them, *"Receive the Holy Spirit. **If you forgive the sins of any, they are forgiven;** if you retain the sins of any, they are retained."* (Jn. 20:21-23)

Today, some mistakenly think that the priest comes between the person and Christ, instead of understanding the priest as a bridge to Christ. Many say: "I want to go directly to Christ not to the priest." However, to go to the priest *is to go directly to Christ* because the priest acts (*in persona Christi*) in the person of Christ, in God's name. *"Peter said, '...you have not lied to men but to God.' When Ananias heard these words, he fell down and died."* (Acts 5:5) The individual priest we confess to is the visible priest, Christ is the invisible priest who is made present and acts through the confessor.

In the year 251 A.D. St. Cyprian of Carthage wrote: "...confess even this to the priests of God in a straight-forward manner and in sorrow, making an open declaration of conscience. Thus they remove the weight from their souls. God cannot be mocked or outwitted; nor can He be deceived by any clever cunning. Indeed, he but sins the more if, thinking that God is like man, he believes that he can escape the punishment of his crime by not openly admitting his crime...I beseech you, brethren, let everyone who has sinned <u>confess</u> his sin while he is still in this world, while his confession is still admissible, while satisfaction and **remission made through the priests are pleasing before the Lord.**" (Rev.W.A. Jurgens, *The Faith of the Early Fathers*, Vol. 1, p. 219)

Some people fear going to confession because of the sacrifice involved in confessing one's sins. This sacrament functions as a tribunal of mercy and a place of spiritual healing; hence, it is necessary for the confessor to have knowledge of the sinner's heart, in order to be able to judge, absolve, cure, and heal. This sacrament involves a sincere and complete confession of sins because of its very nature, as well as an exercise in humility and self-denial. This is one of the hard-earned benefits of confession. We must remember that the road to humility is paved with humiliations. It is a blow to our pride, and a humbling experience for us to go to confession. It is a spiritual growing pain. Jesus says: *"He who exalts himself will be humbled, and he who humbles himself will be exalted."* (Lk. 14:11, 18:14) Pride keeps us from confession. We do not want to humble ourselves before another person, and admit or confess our sins. However, confessing our sins enables us to "get it off our chest", to "let it out", and so it has psychological benefits as well. The advantage of confessing our sins to a priest as opposed to a psychologist or a close friend, is that the priest can give us God's forgiveness as well as man's. When we sin our sins not only affect our relationship with God, but our neighbor. The universe is not just us and God, it is God, my neighbor and myself. Jesus is both God and man. The priest represents both God and man, the Church of Christ and the Christ of the Church. Jesus forgave sins as a man, and men grumbled against Him. What they said about Jesus then, many say about Him now in the person of His priests: *"Why does this man speak thus? It is blasphemy! Who can forgive sins but God alone?"*(Mk. 2:7, Lk. 7:49) Some did not recognize the divinity of Christ under his humble humanity, and today some do not recognize the priesthood of Christ under His humble human instrument, the Catholic Priest.

Scripture says: *"They praised God for giving such authority to* **men**" (Mt. 9:8) *"Christ gave us the ministry of reconciliation...so we are ambassadors for Christ"* (2 Cor. 5:18, 20). We must remember that the Church's power to forgive sins committed after baptism is linked specifically to the priest through the Sacrament of Holy Orders (Mt. 9:8, 18:18, Jn. 20:21-23, Jm. 5:14, 15). The priest is to represent Christ who is both merciful and just. Remember the Proverb: *"He who conceals his sins will not prosper, but he who confesses and forsakes them will obtain mercy."* (Prv. 28:13)

5. **Anointing of the Sick**: [1499-1532] This sacrament forgives sins and may promote physical healing, if it is God's will. *"Is any man sick among you? Let him bring in the priests of the church, and let them pray over him, anointing him with oil in the name of the Lord. And the prayer of faith shall save the sick man: and the Lord shall raise him up: and if he be in sins, they shall be forgiven him."* Jas. 5:13-15 Note—forgiveness of sins in this sacrament, like in confession, is linked with the priest. (Mk. 6:13).

6. **Holy Orders:** [1536-1600] (Gen. 14:18, Heb. 5:5-10, Lk. 22:19, Acts 6:6, 14:22, 23) *"These they set before the Apostles, and they prayed and laid their hands upon them"* (Acts 6:6). This Sacrament comes through the *"laying on of hands"* (1 Tim. 5:22), and enables Christ's apostles and their successors to administer the Sacraments and serve the Church. There are three degrees of Holy Orders: 1. Deacon (1 Tim. 3:8-13), 2. Priest (1 Tim. 5:17-25), 3. Bishop (1 Tim. 3:1-7). Only a bishop (the High Priest) can ordain, and only bishops and priests can administer the sacraments of confirmation, confession, anointing of the sick, and offer the Sacrifice of the Mass. The Ranks of Clergy in descending order are:
   1. **Bishops**: Pope, Cardinal, Archbishop, Bishop, Auxiliary Bishop
   2. **Priests**: Monsignor, Pastor, Assistant Pastor
   3. **Deacons**: permanent and transitional.

A priest is a bridge between heaven and earth. He brings God to man, and brings man to God. A priest is primarily one who offers sacrifice. Christ is both priest and victim, offerer and offering. Christ continues through His Catholic priests, to offer the sacrifice of His Body and Blood, under the appearance of bread and wine, according to the order of Melchizedek.

The first time scripture speaks of priesthood, it is in conjunction with "bread and wine". *"Then Melchizedek, the king of Salem [Jerusalem], brought out bread and wine; for he was a priest of the Most High God."* (Gen.14:18)" *Jesus has...become a high priest forever according to the order of Melchizedek."* (Heb. 6:20, Ps. 110:4)

An altar is a place of sacrifice. Priest and altar go together, *"We have an **altar** from which those who serve the tent have no right to eat."* (Heb.13:10). The Priest offers the body and blood of Christ on the altar. When the priest consecrates the Eucharist and preaches the Gospel he brings God to man; when he forgives sins, he brings man to God. *"Follow me, and I will make you fishers of men."* (Mt. 4:19) *"True instruction was in his mouth, and no wrong was found on his lips. He walked with me in peace and uprightness, and he turned many from iniquity. For the lips of a priest should guard knowledge, and men should seek instructions from his mouth, for he is the messenger of the Lord of hosts."* (Malachi 2:6, 7)

The internal or common priesthood of all the baptized (1 Pt. 2:5, Rev. 1:5, 6) is different from the external or ordained ministerial priesthood given by Christ to administer the sacraments. [CCC 1546-1547]

Why call priests Father?

They are spiritual Fathers in the Church. They give life to people through proclaiming the Gospel and through the Sacraments. (1 Cor. 4:14-15, 1 Thes. 2:9-12, 2 Pt. 3:4)

Why are Latin Rite Priests Celibate?

They follow the example and teaching of Jesus Christ (celibate priest) to sacrifice marriage for the kingdom. (Mt. 19:12, Lk. 18:29, 1 Cor. 7)

7. **Matrimony:** *"What therefore God has joined together, let not man put asunder."* (Mk. 10:2-12, Eph. 5) This Sacrament joins a man and woman together for life by the power of God for the purpose of union (love) and procreation (life). Marriage is binding until death. (1 Cor. 7:10, 11, 39, Mt. 19:4-9). An annulment is a declaration made by the church which states that after a thorough investigation has been completed, the elements necessary for a valid marriage were not present at the time of the wedding, and therefore no true sacramental marriage ever took place (1 Cor. 7:15). It is not a divorce. *"...let none be faithless to the wife of his youth. For I hate divorce, says the Lord."* (Mal. 2:15, 16)

The Crucifixion

And when they came to the place which is called The Skull, there they crucified him, and Jesus said, *"Father, forgive them; for they know not what they do."* (Luke 23:33-34)

Part III

The Commandments

"If you love me, you will keep my commandments." (John 14:15)

The Two Great Commandments:
[2055, 2083]

I. *"You shall love the Lord your God with your whole heart, with your whole soul, and with all your mind. This is the first and greatest commandment. The second is like it."* (Deut. 6:5, Mt. 22:37-39) The first great commandment corresponds to the first 3 of the ten commandments given to Moses.

II. *"You shall love your neighbor as yourself."*(Lev. 18:9, Mt. 22:37-39) The second great commandment corresponds to the last seven commandments.

The Ten Commandments: (Ex. 20:1-17, Deut. 5:6-21)
[2084-2557]

"Enter by the narrow gate; for the gate is wide and the way is easy, that leads to destruction, and those who enter by it are many. For the gate is narrow and the way is hard, that leads to life, and those who find it are few....If you would enter life, keep the commandments." (Mt. 7:13, 14, 19:17-19)

— 47 —

1. *"YOU SHALL HAVE NO FALSE GODS."* [2084-2141] This means we worship only the true God, especially through prayer, and do not give greater love to anything else.

2. *"YOU SHALL NOT TAKE GOD'S NAME IN VAIN."* [2142-2167] Use God's name only with reverence.

3. *"KEEP THE SABBATH HOLY."* [2168-2195] Attend mass on Sundays and Holy Days of obligation, and abstain from unnecessary physical labor on Sunday.

4. *"HONOR YOUR FATHER AND MOTHER."* [2196-2257] Love, help, respect, and obey your parents and legitimate authorities in all things except sin.

5. *"YOU SHALL NOT KILL."* [2258-2330] We must take care of our bodies, and not unjustly injure others physically or verbally (abusive language). (Mt. 5:21-26). Alcohol and drug abuse is sinful (Gal. 5:21). We are allowed to defend ourselves; however, killing out of vengeance is wrong (Rom. 12:19-21). Surgical sterilization for the purpose of contraception, suicide, and euthanasia, are all sinful. Abortion is the murder of innocent life. The eternal soul of a child begins at conception, and the heartbeat of a child begins at 21 days. Abortion stops a beating heart. All souls have a relationship with God, even within the womb. *"...when the voice of your greeting came to my ears,* **the babe in my womb leaped for joy."** (Lk. 1:15, 41, 44) *"Before I formed you in the womb I knew you, and before you were born I consecrated you."* (Jer. 1:5) *"You knit me together in my mother's womb."* (Ps. 139:13) *"They will have no mercy on the fruit of the womb; their eyes will not pity children."* (Is. 13:18) Adoption is a better choice than abortion.

6. *"YOU SHALL NOT COMMIT ADULTERY."* [2331-2400] *"Blessed are the pure in heart, for they shall see God...you have heard that it was said, 'You shall not commit adultery.' But I say to you that every one who looks at a woman lustfully has already committed adultery with her in his heart."* (Mt. 5:8, 27, 28) This commandment calls for the virtue of chastity or purity and forbids all sexual sins: **adultery,**

fornication (pre-marital sex) (Gal. 5:16-24, 1 Cor. 6:15-20, Eph. 5:5, 6, Mt. 15:19, Rev. 22:15), **impure thoughts, pornography** (*"I will not set before my eyes anything that is base."* Ps. 101:3 *"You used your beauty obscenely"* Ezek. 16:25, Mt. 5:27), **immodest Dress** (Is. 3:16-24, 1 Tim. 2:9, 10, 1 Pt. 3:1-6), **masturbation** (Gen. 38:8-10, Mt. 5:30), **homosexual acts** (Gen. 19:1-29, Rom. 1:24-27, 1 Cor .6:10, 1 Tim. 1:10), and **contraception** (Gen. 38:8-10). The Catechism of the Catholic Church calls contraception "intrinsically evil" [2370]. Unlike Natural Family Planning, artificial birth control violates the natural design intended by God for sexuality, for God created conjugal relations to be life-giving. This is God's first blessing— *"And God blessed them, and said, 'Be fruitful and multiply..."* Gen.1:28. Contraception unnaturally separates the two goods of marriage, life (procreation) and love (union) which God by his own authority united: (Gen. 1:28, Ps. 127:3-5, Gen. 38:8-10, Ru. 4:13). *"Has not the one God made and sustained for us the spirit of life? And what does he desire? Godly offspring..."* (Malachi 2:15) We do not have ultimate authority and domain over our bodies. *"Every other sin which a man commits is outside the body; but the immoral man sins against his own body. Do you not know that your body is a temple of the Holy Spirit within you, which you have from God? You are not your own; you were bought with a price. So glorify God in your body."* (1 Cor. 6:15-20) For information contact your local parish or diocesan family planning office.

The sin of fornication (pre-marital sex) is the use of the marital act outside of marriage. It involves not only the act of intercourse, but any sexual touches, passionate kissing for the purpose of arousal, etc. which lead up to the act. Couples who love each other should demonstrate their love by giving themselves to one another through marriage before they give their bodies through sex. True love means "only you and always you", and such a commitment is shown only through marriage. This sin injures body, soul, heart, and mind:

- First, a mortal sin is committed which causes the loss of friendship with God and the loss of eternal life.
- Second, the risk of unwanted pregnancy and the temptation to murder through abortion.
- Third, the risk of venereal disease and AIDS.
- Fourth, the emotional pain of separation occurs after intimate

union without the commitment of marriage.

The virtue of chastity comes only through grace and prayer. It means using our sexual powers according to God's will, and involves abstinence until marriage with faithfulness to your partner in marriage. Remember to go to your parish priest before getting married. If a Catholic marries outside the church it is a sinful and invalid marriage. (CCC 1625-1637)

7. *"YOU SHALL NOT STEAL."* [2401-2463] If one steals one must make restitution and return the property if possible, or give to the poor. However, one can take food to survive when in danger of starvation.

8. *"YOU SHALL NOT BEAR FALSE WITNESS AGAINST YOUR NEIGHBOR."* [2464-2513] Lying, calumny (telling the faults of someone that are untrue), and detraction (unnecessarily revealing someone's true faults) are wrong. *"Do not speak evil against one another, brethren."* (Jm. 4:11) (Eph. 4:29-32)

9. *"YOU SHALL NOT COVET YOUR NEIGHBOR'S WIFE."* [2514-2533] This teaches that willful and deliberate, impure thoughts are sinful (Mt. 5:27, 28), and also immodest dress which can promote impure thoughts.

10. *"YOU SHALL NOT COVET YOUR NEIGHBOR'S GOODS."* [2534-2557] The virtue of detachment is needed to obey this commandment. Scripture warns against attachment to wealth (Mt. 19:16-30, Lk. 6:20-26, 12:13-31, Jm. 5:1-6).

The Six Commandments or Precepts of the Church
[2041-2043, 2048]

1. To attend Mass on all Sundays and Holy Days of Obligation.
2. To fast and abstain on the days appointed.
3. To confess our sins at least once a year.
4. To receive Holy Communion during the Easter Season.
5. To contribute to the support of the Church. (Give alms according to your income to your local church, charities, and missionaries.)

6. To observe the laws of the Church regarding marriage. (Be married only with the Church's permission.)

Holy Days of Obligation
[2043, 2180, 2698]

All Sundays as well as: December 8 - Immaculate Conception, Dec.25 - Christmas, Jan.1 - Solemnity of Mary, Ascension Thursday - 40 days after Easter, August 15 - Assumption of Mary, and Nov.1 - All Saints Day. (In those dioceses which have chosen the option, Ascension is Transferred from Thursday to the Seventh Sunday of Easter.) In the U.S.A., when Jan.1, Aug.15, or Nov. 1, fall on a Saturday or a Monday, there is no obligation to attend Mass.

Sins Against the Holy Spirit
[1864]

1. Presumption.
2. Despair.
3. Resisting the known truth.
4. Envy of another's spiritual good.
5. Obstinacy in sin.
6. Final impenitence.

Virtues and Vices

Virtue: [1804] A good habit; a habit of doing good and avoiding evil.
Vice: [1865] A bad habit; a habit of sin.

Seven Virtues:
[1833-1844]

1. humility
2. detachment
3. chastity
4. brotherly love

5. temperance
6. meekness
7. diligence

Seven Vices:
[1866,1876]

1. pride   4. envy   6. anger
2. avarice   5. gluttony   7. sloth
3. lust

The Three Theological Virtues:
[1812-1829]

1. faith   2. Hope   3. Love
(1 Cor. 13:13)

The Cardinal Virtues:
[1805]

Prudence   Temperance
Fortitude   Justice

The Cross
[617]

The cross is the condition of Christ's discipleship. It includes all the suffering and hardship involved in resisting temptation, keeping the commandments, and doing the physical and spiritual works of mercy. *"If anyone wishes to come after me, let him deny himself, and take up his cross daily, and follow me."* (Lk. 9:23, 1 Cor. 1:18)

Concupiscence
[1264, 1426, 2515]

"...the imagination and thought of man's heart are prone to evil from his youth." (Gen. 8:21) Concupiscence is the inclination toward sin that our nature possesses as a result of original sin. We must struggle to do good with the help of God's grace. (Gen. 6:5, 8:21, Mt. 26:41, Rom. 7:23, 8:6, Gal. 5:17)

Temptation
[2846-2849]

Temptation is the lure of sin which comes from the world, the flesh, and the devil. *"Your adversary the devil prowls around like a roaring lion, seeking some one to devour. Resist him firm in your faith..."* (1 Pt. 5:8, 9) *"Do not love the world or the things in the world. If any one loves the world, love for the Father is not in him. For all that is in the world, the lust of the flesh and the lust of the eyes and the pride of life, is not of the Father but is of the world. And the world passes away, and the lust of it; but he who does the will of God abides for ever."* (1 Jn. 2:15-17). Temptation is not a sin. In fact, if we are tempted, it is a sign that we have not yet sinned. When we are tempted, we should remember to pray, and think about the four last things: death, judgment, heaven, and hell. *"Watch and pray that you may not enter into temptation; the spirit indeed is willing, but the flesh is weak."* (Mt. 26:41). We are not tempted beyond our strength, provided we pray to God for help. *"No temptation has overtaken you that is not common to man. God is faithful, and he will not let you be tempted beyond your strength, but with the temptation will also provide the way of escape, that you may be able to endure it."* (1 Cor. 10:13, also: Gen. 4:6, 7, Jm. 4:6, 7).

Faith and Works
[160-165, 1987-2029, 2443-2449]

Faith is belief in God, and faith is necessary for salvation (Heb. 11:6). *"Faith is the assurance of things hoped for, the evidence of things not seen."* (Heb. 11:1) (1 Jn. 5:4, 5). St. Paul denounces the "works of the law" (Acts 15:1-11, Rom. 3:28-31) meaning circumcision, kosher laws, and Jewish ceremonial laws, but he does not deny the value of the 10 commandments (Gal. 5:19-21) and the 14 works of mercy, as taught by scripture (*For in Christ Jesus neither circumcision nor uncircumcision is of any avail, but faith working through love. Gal. 5:6*). God requires works of mercy to accompany faith, compare Mt. 22:11-13 and Rev. 19:7, 8, also read: Jas. 2:14-26, Mt. 5:17-22, 7:21-23, 16:27, 19:16-19, 25:31-46, Dan. 4:24, Rev. 3:2, 14:13, 19:8, 20:13, 1 Jn. 2:4, Eph. 5:5-7, Gal. 5:16-21, Rm. 8:17. *"Not every one who says to me, 'Lord, Lord,' shall enter the kingdom of heaven, but he who does the will of my*

Father who is in heaven." (Mt. 7:21) *"If you would enter life, keep the commandments."* (Mt. 19:17-19) *"His commandment is this: we are to believe in the name of his Son, Jesus Christ, **and** are to love one another as he commanded us. **Those who keep his commandments remain in him** and he in them."* (1 Jn. 3:23, 24) *"So faith by itself, if it has no works, is dead...You see that a man is justified by works and not by faith alone. For as the body apart from the spirit is dead, so faith apart from works is dead."* (Jm. 2:14-26) We have a *firm hope and confidence* of salvation through our faith in Christ (Rom. 10:9, 10, Jn. 3:16, 5:24, 11:26, 17:3); however, *we cannot be absolutely certain we are saved*— we must hope for the grace of final perseverance: (Mt. 10:22, 24:13, 1 Cor. 4:3-5, 9:26-27, 10:12, Phil. 2:12, 3:10-16, Jn. 15:6, Heb. 6:11-12, 10:26, 2 Tim. 2:12, 13, Ezek. 33:12-20, Rom. 5:2, 8:24-25). A person can receive the gift of salvation through sanctifying grace, and then lose it through mortal sin. (1 Jn. 5:16, 17, Jn .15:6) St. Paul says: *"But I chastise my body, and bring it into subjection: lest perhaps, after I have preached to others, I myself should become lost.* (1 Cor .9:27)

The Fourteen Good Works of Love and Mercy
[2443, 2447]

Truly, I say to you, as you did it to one of the least of these my brethren, you did it to me. (Mt. 25:40)

The Seven Physical Works of Mercy
1. *Feed the hungry.*
2. *Give drink to the thirsty.*
3. *Clothe the naked.*
4. *Shelter the homeless.*
5. *Visit the sick.*
6. *Visit the imprisoned.* (Mt. 25:34-40)
7. *Bury the dead.* (Tb. 1:16, 17, Acts 8:2)

The Seven Spiritual Works of Mercy
1. *Counsel the doubtful* (1 Thess. 5:9-11).
2. *Instruct the ignorant* (Acts 8:35-39).
3. *Convert or admonish the sinner* (Acts 2:40, 41, Jm. 5:19, 20).
4. *Comfort the sorrowful* (Rom. 12:15).

5. *Forgive all injuries* (Mt. 18:21, 22).
6. *Bear wrongs patiently* (1 Cor. 13:5-7).
7. *Pray for the living and the dead* (Jm. 5:16, 2 Mac. 12:46).

The Resurrection

The angel said to the woman, *"Do not be afraid; for I know that you seek Jesus who was crucified. He is not here; for He has risen, as He said."* (Matthew 28:5, 6)

The Ascension

"But you shall receive power when the Holy Spirit has come upon you; and you shall be my witnesses in Jerusalem and in all Judea and Samaria and the end of the earth." And when he had said this, as they were looking on, he was lifted up, and a cloud took him out of their sight. (Acts 1:8, 9)

Part IV
Prayer
[2558-2561]

"And I tell you, ask, and it will be given you; seek, and you will find; knock, and it will be opened to you." (Lk. 11:9)

What is Prayer? Prayer is lifting our hearts and minds to God. Prayer is conversation with God. St. Augustine: "Prayer is the key of Heaven." Prayer is a living relationship between the children of God and their Father. Prayer is the habit of being in the presence of and in communion with the Holy Trinity. Prayer is the way the Holy Spirit, who dwells within us, inspires and helps us in our weakness to pray and love God (Rom. 8:26).

Why do we pray? [2744] We pray so that we can go to heaven. St. Augustine says: "As our body cannot live without nourishment, so our soul cannot spiritually be kept alive without prayer." St. Alphonsus says: "He who prays, is saved; he who prays not, is damned!" Prayer is powerful: *"Those who trust in you cannot be put to shame."* (Dan. 3:40) *"The unceasing prayer of a just man is of great avail."* (Jm. 5:16-18)
     Prayer can change things:
     "In those days Hezekiah became sick and was at the point of death. And Isaiah the prophet...came to him, and said to him," Thus says the Lord, 'Set your house in order; for you shall die, you shall not recover.'"*

Then Hezekiah turned his face to the wall, and prayed to the Lord, saying "Remember now, O Lord, I beseech thee, how I have walked before thee in faithfulness and with a whole heart, and have done what is good in thy sight." And Hezekiah wept bitterly. And before Isaiah had gone out of the middle court, the word of the Lord came to him: "Turn back, and say to Hezekiah the prince of my people, 'Thus says the Lord, the God of David your father: I have heard your prayer, I have seen your tears; behold, I will heal you; on the third day you shall go up to the house of the Lord. And I will add fifteen years to your life. I will deliver you and this city out of the hand of the king of Assyria, and I will defend this city for my own sake and for my servant David's sake.'" (2 Kings 20:1-6), (Jos. 10:12-14, Dan. 6).

Where do we pray? [2691] We may pray at home in our room (Mt. 6:1-6, Mk. 1:35), at Church with our family (Mt. 21:13), while riding in a car or anywhere. Through prayer, we can sanctify idle moments and give that extra free time to God.

The Four Main Purposes of Prayer [2626-2649]
1. Adoration: Proper worship of God due to Him as our Creator.
2. Thanksgiving: Gratefulness to God for His gifts to us.
3. Reparation: To obtain pardon for sins and do penance.
4. Petition: We ask for spiritual and physical goods.
    "Have no anxiety about anything, but in everything by prayer and supplication with thanksgiving let your requests be made known to God. And the peace of God, which passes all understanding, will keep your hearts and your minds in Christ Jesus." (Phil. 4:6, 7)

The Seven Main Qualities of Prayer [2725-2758]
1. Devotion: Putting our hearts into our prayers. (Mt. 15:8)
2. Fervor: An intense desire to serve God. (Lk. 22:43, 44)
3. Perseverance: *"They ought always to pray and not lose heart."* (Lk. 18:1-8, Lk. 11:5-10, Mt. 24:13)
4. Humility: (Jm.. 4:6, Mt. 6:1-6, Lk.18:9-14)
5. Attention: How can we expect God to listen to our prayer, if we are not paying attention to it? (Mt. 6:7, 8) Involuntary distractions in prayer are inevitable, but we should try to minimize them.
6. Faith: *"Those who trust in you cannot be put to shame."* (Dan.3:40;

Mt. l9:26, Heb.11:6)

7. Right Priority: When we pray we need to have the right priority, namely that of God's will over our own (Lk .22:42, Mt. 6:31-33, 16:26). Does God always answer our prayers? **Yes.** There are three answers to prayer-yes, no, and please wait. No prayer is unanswered, and no prayer is unheard.

We should pray at least 5 to 15 minutes everyday. Since God is the most important "person" in our life, we should speak to Him every day. We spend far more time each day pursuing recreation, than we do in strengthening our relationship with God. Our spiritual life is the priority. And, God is certainly more important than anyone or anything else in our life. He deserves a priority of time, "*pray always*" (Lk. 18:1, 1 Thess. 5:17, Eph. 6:18).

Basic Catholic Prayers

The Sign of the Cross
In the name of the Father, and of the Son, and of the Holy Spirit
Amen. (Jn. 14:14, Mt. 28:19)

The Lord's Prayer
[2759-2865]
Our Father who art in heaven, hallowed be Thy name. Thy kingdom come, Thy will be done on earth, as it is in heaven. Give us this day our daily bread. And forgive us our trespasses as we forgive those who trespass against us. And lead us not into temptation, but deliver us from evil. Amen (Mt. 6:9-13)

The Hail Mary
[2673-2682]
Hail Mary, full of grace! The Lord is with thee. Blessed art thou among women, and blessed is the fruit of thy womb, Jesus. Holy Mary Mother of God, pray for us sinners, now and at the hour of our death. Amen. (Based on Lk. 1:28, 42 and tradition)

The Glory Be
Glory be to the Father, and to the Son, and to the Holy Spirit.
As it was in the beginning, is now, and ever shall be, world without end.

Amen. (Based on Matthew 28:19 and tradition)

Act of Contrition
O my God, I am heartily sorry for having offended you, and I detest all my sins, because I dread the loss of heaven and the pains of hell, but most of all because they offend you, my God, who are all good and deserving of all my love. I firmly resolve, with the help of your grace, to confess my sins, to do penance, and to amend my life. Amen. (Based on Psalm 51.)

The Apostles' Creed
I believe in God the Father Almighty, Creator of heaven and earth; and in Jesus Christ, His only Son, Our Lord; Who was conceived by the Holy Spirit, born of the Virgin Mary, suffered under Pontius Pilate, was crucified, died, and was buried. He descended into hell; on the third day He arose again from the dead. He ascended into heaven, and is seated at the right hand of the Father. He will come again to judge the living and the dead. I believe in the Holy Spirit, the Holy Catholic Church, the communion of saints, the forgiveness of sins, the resurrection of the body, and life everlasting. Amen.

Hail Holy Queen
Hail Holy Queen, Mother of Mercy, our life our sweetness and our hope. To Thee do we cry, poor banished children of Eve. To Thee do we send up our sighs, mourning and weeping in this valley of tears. Turn then, most gracious advocate thine eyes of mercy towards us, and after this our exile, show unto us the blessed fruit of Thy womb, Jesus. O clement, O loving, O sweet virgin Mary.

The Memorare
Remember, O most gracious Virgin Mary, that never was it known that anyone who fled to thy protection, implored thy help, or sought thy intercession was left unaided. Inspired with this confidence, I fly unto thee, O Virgin of virgins, my Mother. To thee I come, before thee I stand, sinful and sorrowful. O Mother of the Word Incarnate, despise not my petitions, but in thy mercy hear and answer me. Amen.

Grace Before Meals
*Bless us O Lord, and these Thy gifts which we are about to receive
from Thy bounty, through Christ our Lord. Amen.*

Grace After Meals
*We give Thee thanks, Almighty God, for these and all Thy gifts which
we have received from Thy bounty through Christ our Lord. Amen.*

Prayer to St. Michael the Archangel
*St. Michael the Archangel, defend us in battle; be our defense
against the wickedness and snares of the devil. May God rebuke him, we
humbly pray; and do thou, O prince of the heavenly host, by the power
of God, cast into hell Satan and all the other evil spirits who prowl about
the world seeking the ruin of souls. Amen.*

Prayer to My Guardian Angel
*Angel of God, my guardian dear
To whom His love commits me here,
Ever this day be at my side,
To light and guard, to rule and guide. Amen.*

Sacramentals
[1667-1668, 1670, 1677]
The Church has instituted Sacramentals. They are sacred signs
which bear a resemblance to the sacraments. They signify effects,
especially of a spiritual nature, which occur through the intercession of
the Church. They help dispose us to receive the sacraments, and help
render various occasions in life holy. The Rosary and the Miraculous
Medal are two of the most popular Sacramentals.

Why Pray The Rosary?
[971, 2678, 2708]

The main devotion to Mary is the Rosary, a Christ-centered, biblical
prayer which combines meditation on the life of Jesus and Mary with
the Lord's prayer and the Hail Mary. Pope John Paul II: "The Rosary
is my favourite prayer...To recite the Rosary is nothing other than to
contemplate with Mary the face of Christ." (Rosarium Virginis Mariae)

In his last year of the seminary, Father Patrick Peyton was dying of tuberculosis, and he prayed the rosary asking for a cure. He recovered fully and went on to start "The Family Rosary Crusade" whose motto was: "The family that prays together stays together". "...there is no problem, no matter how difficult it is, temporal or especially spiritual... that cannot be solved by the Rosary." (Sister Lucia of Fatima to Father Fuentes, 1957)

Jesus taught us that we need to pay attention to the words we speak to God in prayer, and not simply say many words (Mt. 6:7). However, the Bible teaches repetitious prayer is good, see: Mt. 26:44, Psalms 117, 136, 150, Is. 6:3, Rev. 4:8 and Daniel 3:52-90.

We pray to Mary because she is the Mother of God and her prayers are the most powerful. When we pray the Hail Mary we combine worship of God and honor of Mary. We unite our prayers to God with hers.

When we need help most, we don't just go directly to God alone, we ask others to pray for us and with us. When we pray the Rosary, we have Mary, the Holy Mother of God, pray to God for us and with us. God wishes us to honor Mary because of her special role in God's plan of salvation to contribute to the redemption of man, just as much as Eve contributed to the fall of man. Mary is our spiritual Mother, and we grow in grace when we honor her in a spiritual way. *"Whoever glorifies his mother is like one who lays up treasure"* (Sir. 3:4, 5). Just as a Father is filled with joy at the love and respect others give to his children, so too, is God the Father overjoyed and seeks for us to honor His Daughter Mary, the mother of His Son Jesus, and the Mother of His Mystical Body, the Church.

We meditate on the Mysteries of the Rosary by using our imagination to picture each event occurring in front of us as we say the Hail Mary prayers. We should begin to pray the Rosary on a daily basis by praying just a decade each day, until we feel we want to pray more. All who pray the Rosary should experience a profound outpouring of grace. I have a saying, "A decade a day keeps the devil away!"

How to Pray the Rosary

1. Make the Sign of the Cross.
2. Pray the Apostles' Creed on the crucifix.
3. Pray the Lord's prayer on the first bead.
4. Pray the Hail Mary prayer on the next three beads.(The three beads

are a symbol for the Trinity).

5. Pray the Glory Be, and announce the first mystery.(Mysteries are listed below.)
6. Pray the Lord's prayer on the next bead.
7. Pray ten Hail Mary's on the next ten beads while meditating on the mystery.
8. Repeat steps 5-7 again on each remaining decade. (Decade meaning the ten Hail Mary's, Glory be and the Our Father, with the mystery.)
9. End by praying the Hail Holy Queen.

People usually say 5 Decades of the Rosary a day. If you find the Rosary too hard at first or don't seem to have the time, then you should start off with 1 decade a day. You may later want to pray 5 decades a day as you get used to the prayer.

The Mysteries of the Rosary

To meditate on the Mysteries we can use pictures, or use our imagination to picture the scene in our minds.

The Joyful Mysteries:
(Usually said on Monday and Thursday)
1. The Annunciation (Lk. 1:28—For humility)
2. The Visitation (Lk. 1:41-42—For Love of Neighbor)
3. The Nativity (Lk. 2:7—For Poverty)
4. The Presentation (Lk. 2:22-23—For Obedience)
5. The Finding in the Temple (Lk. 2:46—For Joy in Finding Jesus)

The Luminous Mysteries:
(Usually said on Thursdays)
6. The Baptism of Jesus (Mt. 3:16-17—For Openness to the Holy Spirit)
7. The Wedding at Cana (Jn. 2:5-7—To Jesus Through Mary)
8. Proclaiming the Kingdom (Mt. 10:7-8—Repentance and Trust in God)
9. The Transfiguration (Lk. 9:29-35—Desire for Holiness)
10. The Institution of the Eucharist (Lk. 22:19-20-Adoration)

The Sorrowful Mysteries:
(Usually said on Tuesday and Friday)
11. The Agony in the Garden (Lk. 22:44-45—For sorrow for sin)
12. The Scourging at the Pillar (Jn. 19:1—For purity)

13. The Crowning with Thorns (Mt. 27:28-29—For courage)
14. The Carrying of the Cross (Jn .19:17—For Patience)
15. The Crucifixion (Lk. 23:46—For Perseverance)

The Glorious Mysteries:
(Usually said on Wednesday, Saturday, and Sunday)
16. The Resurrection (Mk. 16:6—For Faith)
17. The Ascension (Mk. 16:19—For Hope)
18. The Descent of the Holy Spirit (Acts 2:4—For Love of God)
19. The Assumption of Mary (Rev. 21:1—For a happy death)
20. The Coronation of Mary (Rev. 21:1—For trust in Mary's
Intercession)

The Fifteen Promises of the Rosary
These are the Fifteen Promises of Mary to Christians who pray the
Rosary. They were given in a private revelation to St. Dominic and
Blessed Alan.
1. Whoever will faithfully serve me by the recitation of the Rosary will
receive signal graces.
2. I promise my special protection and greatest graces to all those who
will recite the Rosary.
3. The Rosary shall be a powerful armor against Hell: it shall destroy
vice, decrease sin, and defeat heresies.
4. I will cause virtue and good works to flourish; it shall obtain for
souls the abundant mercy of God; it shall withdraw the hearts of men
from the love of the world and its vanities and shall lift them to the
desire of eternal things. Oh, that souls would sanctify themselves by
this means!
5. The soul that recommends itself to me by the meditation of the
Rosary shall not perish.
6. Whoever will recite the Rosary devoutly, applying himself to the
consideration of its sacred mysteries, shall never be conquered by
misfortune. God will not chastise him in His justice; he shall not
perish by an unprovided death; if he shall be just, he shall remain in
the grace of God and become worthy of eternal life.
7. Whoever will have a true devotion for the Rosary shall not die
without the sacraments of the Church.
8. Those who faithfully recite the Rosary shall have during their life

and at their death the light of God and the plentitude of His graces; at the moment of death they shall participate in the merits of the saints in paradise.

9. I will deliver from purgatory those who have been devoted to the Rosary.
10. The faithful children of the Rosary shall merit a high degree of glory in heaven.
11. You shall obtain all that you ask of me by the recitation of the Rosary.
12. All those who propagate the holy Rosary shall be aided by me in their necessities.
13. I have obtained from my divine Son that all the advocates of the Rosary shall have for intercessors the entire celestial court during their life and at the hour of their death.
14. All who recite the Rosary are my sons and brothers of my only Son, Jesus Christ.
15. Devotion to the Rosary is a great sign of predestination.(Imprimatur for 15 Promises was given by Patrick J.Hayes, D.D., Archbishop of New York)

The Miraculous Medal

The Blessed Virgin Mary spoke to St.Catherine Laboure on November 27, 1830, saying: *"Have a medal struck after this image. All who wear it will receive great graces; they should wear it around the neck. Graces will abound for those who wear it with confidence."* In 1832 the first medals were being distributed in France with the church's approval. As a result of the many miracles both spiritual and physical—conversions, healings, and protection from injuries—it quickly became known as "The Miraculous Medal". These miracles have continued since the Medal was first propagated in 1832. People who have worn the medal have become more receptive to God's grace. The medal is not magical; God has chosen to use this medal as an instrument to bring His grace to us. It is similar to the Rod of Moses (Ex. 14:15-31), the Serpent of Brass (Num. 21:8, 9) and the handkerchief of St. Paul (Acts 19:11-12). The Woman on the front of the Medal is Mary, and she is like the Woman in Rev. 12:1: *"A great sign appeared in the heavens, a woman clothed with the sun."* A serpent who seduced Eve, is under her feet symbolizing the prophesy in Gen. 3:15. Unlike Eve, Mary defeats the serpent because she never committed sin. The Medal reads *"O Mary Conceived without sin pray for us who have recourse to thee*". We should try to pray this prayer each day. The twelve stars symbolize the crown of Mary in Rev.12:1 "*On her head a crown of 12 stars*", also the 12 tribes of Israel, the 12 Apostles, and the 12 fruits of the Holy Spirit (Gal. 5:22). The hearts on the medal symbolize the Sacred Heart of Jesus (Mt. 11:29, Jn. 13:23) and the Immaculate Heart of Mary (Lk. 2:19, 35, 51), which has a sword through it symbolizing her sorrow over the death of her Son and the sins of the world. The Cross with the Letter M for Mary, symbolizes how Mary and Jesus work together for our redemption as Adam and Eve acted together for our fall from grace. The rays from her hands symbolize the graces that fall from heaven to earth, especially those which people ask for.

Pentecost

And there appeared to them tongues as of fire, distributed and resting on each one of them, and they were all filled wth the Holy Spirit and began to speak in other tongues, as the Spirit gave them utterance. (Acts 1:3, 4)

Indulgences

"Now I rejoice in my sufferings for your sake, and in my flesh I complete what is lacking in Christ's afflictions for the sake of his body, that is, the church..." (Col. 1:24)

Excerpt from "Catechism of the Catholic Church":
1471 The doctrine and practice of indulgences in the Church are closely linked to the effects of the sacrament of Penance.

What is an indulgence?

"An indulgence is a remission before God of the temporal punishment due to sins whose guilt has already been forgiven, which the faithful Christian who is duly disposed gains under certain prescribed conditions through the action of the Church which, as the minister of redemption, dispenses and applies with authority the treasury of the satisfaction of Christ and the saints."

"An indulgence is partial or plenary according as it removes either part or all of the temporal punishment due to sin." The faithful can gain indulgences for themselves or apply them to the dead.

—Taken from "Catechism of the Catholic Church" English Edition.

The following excerpts are from *The Handbook of Indulgences, Norms and Grants*, Third Edition 1986. This book lists requirements for gaining indulgences and different prayers and pious actions which bring indulgences.

"...Beside the exclusion of all attachment to sin, even venial sin, the requirements for gaining a plenary indulgence are the performance of the indulgenced work and fulfillment of three conditions: sacramental confession, eucharistic communion, and prayer for the Pope's intentions...The condition requiring prayer for the pope's intentions is satisfied by reciting once the Our Father and Hail Mary for his intentions; nevertheless all the faithful have the option of reciting any other prayer suited to their own piety and devotion..." Pp. 22, 23.

Adoration of the Blessed Sacrament

A partial indulgence is granted the Christian faithful when they visit the Blessed Sacrament for the purpose of adoration. When this is done for at least half an hour, the indulgence is a plenary one. P. 40.

Recitation of the Marian Rosary

A plenary indulgence is granted when the rosary is recited in a church or oratory or when it is recited in a family, a religious community, or a pious association. A partial indulgence is granted for its recitation in all other circumstances. P. 79.

The Handbook of Indulgences, Norms and Grants, Authorized English Edition, Copyright 1991, Catholic Book Publishing Co., N.Y.

The Stations of the Cross:

Mary and the Apostles walked through the streets of Jerusalem and recalled the sufferings Our Lord endured there. The Stations in the Church represent these places on the road to Calvary. Meditating on His Passion helps us grow in our love for Christ and sorrow for our sins which crucified him. To gain a plenary indulgence from the stations one must devoutly make the Stations of the Cross meditating on the passion and death of the Lord. No additional prayers are required. The stations of the Cross are usually prayed publicly on Fridays during Lent, but they can be prayed privately anytime during the year. The Stations are as follows:

1. Jesus is condemned to death by Pilate. (Lk. 23:24)
2. Jesus takes up His cross. (Jn. 19:17)
3. Jesus falls for the first time.
4. Jesus meets His sorrowful mother.
5. Jesus is assisted by Simon the Cyrene. (Lk. 23:26)
6. Veronica wipes the face of Jesus with her veil.
7. Jesus falls the second time.
8. Jesus meets the sorrowful women. (Lk. 23:27-31)
9. Jesus falls the third time.
10. Jesus is stripped of His garments. (Jn. 19:23-24)
11. Jesus is nailed to the cross.

12. Jesus dies on the cross. (Jn. 19:30)
13. Jesus is taken down from the cross.
14. Jesus is laid in the tomb. (Jn. 19:42)

The Brown Scapular

A most Popular Sacramental is the Brown Scapular.

"Whosoever dies wearing this Scapular, shall not suffer eternal fire." Our Lady of Mt. Carmel to St. Simon Stock, July 16, 1251.

"The Scapular will be for all the sign of our Consecration to the Immaculate Heart of Mary." Pope Pius XII

Any priest may bless and enroll a person in the Brown Scapular. The Sabbatine Privilege consists of Our Lady's promise to release from Purgatory, through her special intercession, on the first Saturday after their death, those who meet these three requirements:
1. Wear the Scapular.
2. Observe Chastity according to your state in life.
3. Pray daily the Little Office of Our Lady or substitute the Rosary with permission of a confessor. All confessors were given faculty to make this substitution by Pope Leo XIII in June 1901.

The Prayer of St. Francis

Lord, make me an instrument of your peace.
Where there is hatred, let me sow love.
Where there is injury, pardon.
Where there is doubt, faith.
Where there is despair, hope.
Where there is darkness, light.
And, where there is sadness, joy.
Divine Master, grant that I may not so much seek
to be consoled, as to console;
to be understood as to understand;
to be loved as to love.
For it is in giving that we receive.

It is in pardoning that we are pardoned;
and it is in dying that we are born to eternal life.

The Prayer of St. Patrick (433 A.D.)
(Abridged)

I arise today—
in the strong power of an invocation of the Trinity,
through faith in the Three Persons,
through confession of the oneness,
of the creator of the Universe.

I arise today through -
God's power to lead me,
God's might to uphold me,
God's Wisdom to teach me,
God's eye to watch over me,
God's Ear to hear me,
God's Word to give me speech,
God's Hand to guide me,
God's Way to lie before me,
God's Shield to protect me,
God's Host to save me.

I pray—
Christ with me, Christ before me,
Christ behind me, Christ within me,
Christ beneath me, Christ above me,
Christ at my right side, Christ at me left side,
Christ in my lying down, Christ in my sitting,
Christ in my rising up.
Christ in the heart of every man who thinks of me,
Christ in the mouth of every man who speaks to me,
Christ in every eye that sees me,
Christ in every ear that hears me.

Anima Christi

Soul of Christ, sanctify me.
Body of Christ, save me.
Blood of Christ, inebriate me.
Water from the side of Christ, wash me.
Passion of Christ strengthen me.
O good Jesus, hear me.
Within Your wounds, hide me.
Never permit me to be separated from You.
From the evil one, protect me.
At the hour of my death, call me.
And bid me come to You
That with Your saints I may praise You, forever. Amen.

By St. Ignatius of Loyola—traditionally prayed after Holy Communion.

The Divine Praises

Blessed be God.
Blessed be His holy name.
Blessed be Jesus Christ, true God and true man.
Blessed be the name of Jesus.
Blessed be His most Sacred Heart
Blessed be His most Precious Blood.
Blessed be Jesus in the most Holy Sacrament of the Altar.
Blessed be the Holy Spirit, the Paraclete.
Blessed be the great Mother of God, Mary most holy.
Blessed be her holy and Immaculate Conception.
Blessed be her glorious Assumption.
Blessed be the name of Mary, Virgin and Mother.
Blessed be Saint Joseph, her most chaste spouse.
Blessed be God in His angels and in His saints.

The Angelus

V.　*The angel of the Lord declared unto Mary.*
R.　*And she conceived by the Holy Spirit.* (Mt. 1:20)
　　Hail Mary... (Lk. 1:28, 42)
V.　*Behold the handmaid of the Lord.* (Lk. 1:38)
R.　*Be it done unto me according to Thy word.* (Lk. 1:38)
　　Hail Mary...
V.　*And the Word was made flesh.* (Jn. 1:14)
R.　*And dwelt among us.* (Jn. 1:14)
　　Hail Mary...
V.　*Pray for us, O holy Mother of God.*
R.　*That we may be made worthy of the promises of Christ.*

Let us pray: Pour forth, we beseech Thee, O Lord, Thy grace into our hearts: that we to whom the Incarnation of Christ, Thy Son, was made known by the message of an angel, may by His Passion and Cross, be brought to the glory of His Resurrection through the same Christ our Lord. Amen. (*Note the Angelus is traditionally said by families and friends who are together at 12 and 6 PM.)

The Regina Caeli

(Said during Eastertime, instead of The Angelus)
Queen of Heaven, rejoice, Alleluia. (Rev. 12:1)
For He whom thou didst deserve to bear, Alleluia.
Hath risen as He said, Alleluia. (Mt. 28:6)
Pray for us to God, Alleluia.
V.　*Rejoice and be glad, O Virgin Mary! Alleluia.*
R.　*Because the Lord is truly Risen, Alleluia.*

Let us pray: O God, Who, by the resurrection of Thy Son, Our Lord Jesus Christ, hast vouchsafed to make glad the whole world; grant, we beseech Thee, that through the intercession of the Virgin Mary, His Mother, we may attain the joys of eternal life. Through the same Christ Our Lord. Amen.

The Fatima Prayer:

O my Jesus, forgive us our sins, save us from the fires of hell, lead all souls to heaven, especially those in most need of thy mercy. (This prayer was given in a private apparition by Our Lady of Fatima who requested it be added to the Rosary after each "Glory Be".)

St. Teresa's Meditation

Let nothing disturb you.
Let nothing frighten you.
All things are passing;
God never changes.
Patient endurance obtains all things;
He who has God has everything.
God alone suffices.

The Parable of Nature
(Rom. 1:19, 20/Wis. 13:5)

His eyes twinkle in the stars, and His face smiles in the flower.

I behold His beauty in the sunset, and His golden hair in the wheat of the field.

I hear the Almighty's voice in the thunder, and sense His anger in the storm.

Observe the Lord's tears in the rain, and share His cheer in the sun shower.

Envision His arm in the lightning, and His finger in the eclipse.

One can feel His breath in the wind, and His sweat in the ocean spray.

Notice His shoulders in the hills, His footprints in the valleys.

We understand His depth in the ocean, and heights of divinity in the heavens.

I touch His solidity in the firmness of rocks.

I can taste divine sweetness in the fruit of the tree and vine,

I smell His aroma in the flowers and the pines.

In the clouds we picture the heavenly clothing and the supreme colors in autumn leaves.

I behold the Lord's throne in the mountains and His staff in the trees.

I see the Heavenly Father's robe in the northern lights, and His belt in the rainbow.

One can recognize divine purity in the sparkling of ice, and the riches of divinity in the earth's minerals.

Consider the stillness of the Almighty in the eye of a hurricane, or His majestic speed in the tornado.

Men encounter His moods in the seasons, and His mystery in the light of the moon.

I detect the passing of the Lord's Spirit in the twilight, and the coming of His justice with the dawn.

I discern the secrets of the Lord's salvation in the seed which dies to become a new life (Jn. 12:24) — *for the parable of nature is the reflection of God.* — *Poem by Fr. Herbert Burke*

A Mini History of the Church

"Remember your leaders, who spoke to you the word of God Consider how they ended their lives, and imitate their faith."
(Hebrews 13:7)

33 A.D. Our Lord dies on the cross, and rises from the dead.

33 A.D. Pentecost, the Catholic Church is born (Acts 2).

36 A.D. St. Stephen is stoned to death becoming the first martyr.

51 A.D. First Church Council is held in Jerusalem, presided over by the First Pope St. Peter, who settles the first doctrinal dispute (Acts 15:7-12). This shows the biblical model the Catholic Church uses, following the decisions of Peter and his successors.

64-68 A.D. First persecution of Christians by the Emperor Nero.

67 A.D. The martyrdom of Sts. Peter and Paul. (June 29th)

70 A.D. The Destruction of the Temple as predicted in Lk.18:41-44

42 A.D. to 104 A.D. Eleven Apostles are martyred.

107 A.D. Martyrdom of St. Ignatius of Antioch, Bishop of Antioch; he was eaten by lions. His writings are the first which call the church "Catholic", he wrote, "Where Jesus is, there is the Catholic Church." His feast is October 17th.

54-305 A.D. The Ten Great Roman Persecutions—Emperor Nero, 54-68 A.D., to the Emperor Diocletian, 284-305 A.D. During these persecutions Christians were brutally tortured and martyred, yet the Catholic Church continued to preach the Gospel and gain more converts.

313 A.D. Edict of Milan—The Roman persecutions are ended.

325 A.D. The Council of Nicea—Defines The Trinity.

389-461 A.D. St. Patrick brings the Gospel to Ireland (Mar. 17).

431 A.D. The Council of Ephesus declared Mary "Mother of God."

452 A.D. Pope St. Leo the Great (Nov. 10) meets Attila the Hun face to face and convinces him not to destroy Rome.

480-547 A.D. St. Benedict, the Father of Western Monasticism, founded the Benedictine Monks. Their motto: "Pray and labor".

521-597 A.D. St. Columba converted Scotland.(June 9).

604 A.D. St. Augustine of Canterbury was sent by Pope St. Gregory the Great to evangelize England. Patron of England (May 27).

722 A.D. St. Boniface goes on his mission to convert Germany. He is the Patron Saint of Germany. (June 5)

732 A.D. The Moslem attack is stopped at the Battle of Tours.

826 A.D. St. Ansgar, "Apostle of the North" (Scandanavia). (Feb. 3)

825-69 A.D. Sts. Cyril and Methodius convert the Slavs. (Feb. 14)

1030-79 A.D. St. Stanislaus, Bishop of Cracow, is martyred. (April 11)

1054 A.D. Greek Schism occurs from a dispute over the Papacy.

1170-1221 A.D. St. Dominic founds the Dominican Order. (August 8)

1082 A.D. St. Bruno founds the Carthusian Order of Hermits. (Oct. 6)

1181-1226 A.D. St. Francis of Assisi. While praying in a ruined Church he heard Our Lord speak to him from the crucifix: *"Francis my house is falling into ruin, rebuild it"*. He sought to rebuild the old church, but later realized our Lord meant to rebuild the spirituality of the people. His holiness attracted many disciples who were the beginnings of the Order of St. Francis. (Oct. 4)

1225-1274 A.D. St.Thomas Aquinas, Doctor of the Church, combined the philosophy of Aristotle with Catholic theology. His writings exhibit the profound unity of faith and reason. (Jan. 28)

1492 A.D. Christopher Columbus discovers America.

1517 A.D. Father Martin Luther, an Augustinian priest, proposes a misinterpretation of Romans that a man is saved by "faith alone", without charitable works or the 10 commandments. The Church disagrees (Mt. 7:21-23, 19:17-19, Gal. 5:16-21, Jm. 2:14-26). He added the word "alone" to his German Translation. This conflict results in a split in the church with many offshoots. The Second Vatican Council (1962) later acknowledged that Catholic and Protestant "men of both sides were to blame." (Unitatis Redintegratio) for the split of Christianity, and called for Ecumenism.

1531 A.D. Our Lady of Guadalupe appeared to an Indian convert, St. Juan Diego. Mary leaves a Miraculous Image of Herself, on display in Mexico, that still baffles scientists of our day. (Dec. 12)

1535 A.D. St. Thomas More and, St. John Fisher, were martyred by King Henry VIII because they refused to recognize the king, instead of the Pope, as head of the Church in England. (June 22)

1545-1563 A.D. The Council of Trent contradicts Protestantism. It teaches how man is justified by grace, but not faith without obedience. Charitable works and obedience to God's commandments begin and end in grace, and are a necessity for salvation.

1491-1556 A.D. St. Ignatius Loyola founds the Jesuits. (July 31)

1506-1552 A.D. St. Francis Xavier brought the gospel to Japan, the Philippines, and New Guinea. *"As long as there are souls in the world who do not love God I cannot rest."* (December 3)

1566-1597 A.D. St. Paul Miki and 25 companions were martyred by crucifixion in Nagasaki during the persecution by the Emperor. (Feb. 6)

The Cloth of Our Lady of Guadalupe

Now a great sign appeared in heaven: a woman, adorned with the sun, standing on the moon and with twelve stars on her head for a crown... Then the dragon was enraged with the woman and went away to make war on the rest of her children, that is, all who obey God's commandments and bear witness for Jesus. (Rev. 12:1, 17)

— 77 —

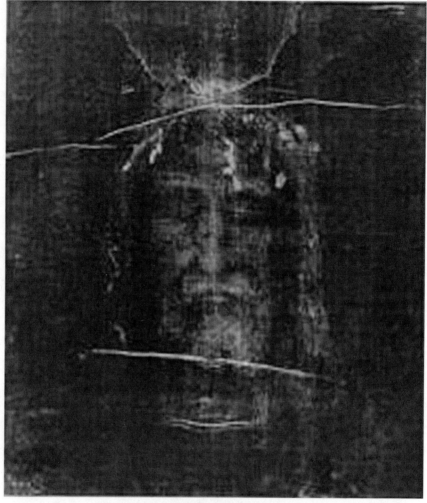

The Mysterious Shroud of Turin

The Disciples reached the tomb bent down and saw the linen cloths lying on the ground but did not go in. Simon Peter who was following came up, went right into the tomb, and saw the linen cloths on the ground. And also the cloth that had been over his head. It was not with the linen cloths but rolled up in a place by itself. (Jn. 20:6, 7)

1624 A.D. Alexander de Thodes, S.J., the "Apostle of Vietnam", converted many. Persecutions of Catholics later came, and there were 117 beatified as the "Martyrs of Tonkin."

1607-1646 A.D. St. Isaac Jogues, a Jesuit missionary was martyred by Mohawks near Albany, New York. (October 19)

1656-1680 A.D. Bl. Kateri Tekakwitha, "the Lily of the Mohawks", was an Indian convert who excelled in virtue. (July 14)

1647-1690 A.D. St. Margaret Mary Alacoque received the visions of the Sacred Heart of Our Lord. (Oct.16)

1769 A.D. Bl. Junipero Serra starts a mission at San Diego (July 1).

1774-1821 St. Elizabeth Ann Seton, first American Saint (Jan. 4).

1786-1859 A.D. Holy St. John Vianney told people their sins in confession before they told him. Patron of Parish Priests (Aug 4)

1806-76 A.D. St. Catherine Laboure receives the Miraculous Medal.

1839-1846 A.D. The 79 Martyrs of Korea. (Sept. 20)

1844-79 A.D. Our Lady appears to St. Bernadette in Lourdes, France, and directs her to a spring; miraculous healings have been attributed to it ever since. Our Lady told her, *"I do not promise to make you happy in this world, but in the next."* St. Bernadette's feast is April 16. Our Lady of Lourdes is Feb. 11.

1854 A.D. Dec. 8 Pope Pius IX—Dogma of Immaculate Conception.

1869-71 A.D. Vatican I teaches Papal Infallibility.

1889-1956 A.D. 119 are martyred in China. Persecution of Catholics in China continues to this day under the Communists. (July 9)

1890-1902 A.D St. Maria Goretti, virgin and martyr, was only 12 years old when she gave her life for Christ. A man tried to seduce her but she refused him and was stabbed to death. (July 6)

1917 A.D. The Russian Communist Revolution occurs. Communism comes to Russia, and Catholics are persecuted for their faith.

1917 A.D. Our Lady of Fatima appears to three children in Portugal six times between May 13 and Oct.13. Our Lady requested that people pray the rosary daily and do penance for the conversion of sinners and the conversion of Russia.

1894-1941 A.D. St. Maximilian Kolbe, a Polish born Priest who was a prisoner in Auschwitz, offered his life to the Nazis in exchange for the life of a married man with a family. (Aug.14)

1949 A.D. The Chinese Communist Revolution occurs and outlaws the Roman Catholic Religion.

1951 A.D. Archbishop Fulton J. Sheen becomes the first Christian Minister to have a TV show, it's called, "Life is Worth Living."

1962-65 A.D. The Council of Vatican II calls for Reforms in the liturgy. The Church later allows translations of the revised Latin mass to the vernacular or native tongue. It calls for a new dialogue of ecumenism with the Orthodox and the Protestants, who are now to be called "separated brethren." It also reaffirms the Church's teaching on celibacy for the priesthood, and the sins of contraception (GS51) and abortion (GS51).

1963 A.D. U.S. Supreme Court forces prayer out of public schools.

1968 A.D. Pope Paul VI reaffirms Church's teaching against contraception in his Encyclical "Humanae Vitae."

1969 A.D. The evil of hardcore pornography begins in America.

1973 A.D. *Roe v. Wade* decision: The Supreme Court in the U.S. allows abortion to be performed through the full 9 months of pregnancy. Each year in our nation's capital on January 22 the March for Life is held to protest the death of the unborn.

1992 A.D. The "Catechism of the Catholic Church" is issued by Pope John Paul II. All catechisms are to be in conformity with it.

The Twelve Promises of the Sacred Heart

Given by Our Lord in a private revelation to St. Margaret Mary Alacoque in 1675:

1. *I will give them all the graces necessary in their state in life.*
2. *I will establish peace in their homes.*
3. *I will comfort them in all their afflictions.*
4. *I will be their secure refuge during life and, above all, in death.*
5. *I will bestow abundant blessings upon all their undertakings.*

Prayer

6. Sinners shall find in My Heart the source and the infinite ocean of mercy.
7. By devotion to My Heart tepid souls shall grow fervent.
8. Fervent souls shall quickly mount to high perfection.
9. I will bless every place where a picture of My Heart shall be set up and honored.
10. I will give to priests the gift of touching the most hardened hearts.
11. Those who promote this devotion shall have their names written in My Heart, never to be blotted out.
12. I will grant the grace of final penitence to those who receive Holy Communion on the first Friday of nine consecutive months.

The Litany of the Sacred Heart

"Come to me, all who labor and are heavy laden, and I will give you rest. Take my yoke upon you, and learn from me; for I am gentle and lowly in heart, and you will find rest for your souls. For my yoke is easy, and my burden light." Mt. 11:28-30

Voice:	*Response:*
Lord, have mercy,	*Lord, have mercy*
Christ, have mercy	*Christ, have mercy*
Lord, have mercy	*Lord, have mercy*
God our Father in heaven	*have mercy on us*
God the Son, Redeemer of the world	*have mercy on us*
God the Holy Spirit	*have mercy on us*
Holy Trinity, one God	*have mercy on us*
Heart of Jesus, Son of the eternal Father	*have mercy on us*
Heart of Jesus, formed by the Holy Spirit in the womb of the Virgin Mother	*have mercy on us*
Heart of Jesus, one with the eternal Word	*have mercy on us*
Heart of Jesus, infinite in majesty	*have mercy on us*
Heart of Jesus, holy temple of God	*have mercy on us*
Heart of Jesus, tabernacle of the Most High	*have mercy on us*
Heart of Jesus, house of God and gate of heaven	*have mercy on us*
Heart of Jesus, aflame with love for us	*have mercy on us*
Heart of Jesus, source of justice and love	*have mercy on us*
Heart of Jesus, full of goodness and love	*have mercy on us*

Heart of Jesus, well-spring of all virtue	*have mercy on us*
Heart of Jesus, worthy of all praise	*have mercy on us*
Heart of Jesus, king and center of all hearts	*have mercy on us*
and knowledge	*have mercy on us*
Heart of Jesus, in whom there dwells the	
fullness of divinity	*have mercy on us*
Heart of Jesus, in whom the Father is well pleased	*have mercy on us*
Heart of Jesus, from whose fullness we	
have all received	*have mercy on us*
Heart of Jesus, desire of the eternal hills	*have mercy on us*
Heart of Jesus, patient and full of mercy	*have mercy on us*
Heart of Jesus, generous to all who turn to you	*have mercy on us*
Heart of Jesus, fountain of life and holiness	*have mercy on us*
Heart of Jesus, atonement for our sins	*have mercy on us*
Heart of Jesus, overwhelmed with insults	*have mercy on us*
Heart of Jesus, broken for our sins	*have mercy on us*
Heart of Jesus, obedient even to death	*have mercy on us*
Heart of Jesus, pierced by a lance	*have mercy on us*
Heart of Jesus, source of all consolation	*have mercy on us*
Heart of Jesus, our life and resurrection	*have mercy on us*
Heart of Jesus, our peace and reconciliation	*have mercy on us*
Heart of Jesus, victim for our sins	*have mercy on us*
Heart of Jesus, salvation of all who trust in you	*have mercy on us*
Heart of Jesus, hope of all who die in you	*have mercy on us*
Heart of Jesus, delight of all the saints	*have mercy on us*
Lamb of God, you take away the sins of the world	*have mercy on us*
Lamb of God, you take away the sins of the world	*have mercy on us*
Lamb of God, you take away the sins of the world	*have mercy on us*
V. Jesus, gentle and humble of heart.	
R. Touch our hearts and make them like yours	*have mercy on us*

Let us pray.
Father, we rejoice in the gifts of love we have
received from the heart of Jesus your Son.
Open our hearts to share his life
and continue to bless us with his love.
We ask this in the name of Jesus the Lord.

R. Amen.

Discussion Questions

1. Give one quote from scripture that tells us why we are here or what the purpose of life is? Pp. 1-2
2. Divine Revelation comes down to us through what two sources? P. 8
3. Explain the Mystery of the Holy Trinity as best you can? Pp. 10-11
4. Why can't we use the Bible only to learn about God? P. 9
5. What is one reason God allows evil? Pp. 5-7
6. What are some of the attributes or qualities of God? P. 10
7. Is Jesus both God and Man? What did he do for our salvation? P. 11
8. How many of the Seven Gifts and Twelve Fruits of the Holy Spirit can you name from memory? P. 12
9. Does everyone have a guardian angel? P. 14
10. What kind of grace do we need to get into heaven? P. 16
11. What does original sin do to us? P. 16
12. What is sin? P. 16
13. What are the three conditions of a mortal sin? Pp. 16-17
14. What are the four marks of the Church? P. 18
15. What does the word "Pope" mean and what is his job? P. 18
16. What is the Immaculate Conception? P. 22
17. Do we worship or honor Mary as our Spiritual Mother? P. 24
18. What is a sacrament? P. 31
19. Can you name the seven sacraments from memory? Pp. 31-45
20. What do baptism and confirmation do for the soul, and can they be received more than once? Pp. 31, 32
21. Is it a sin to deliberately conceal a mortal sin in confession? P. 41
22. The priest cannot tell other people the sins you confess, and this is called the? P. 40
23. What is the difference between imperfect and perfect contrition? P. 41
24. At the consecration of the mass the substance of bread and wine is changed into the body, blood, soul, and divinity of Christ. This change is called? P. 33
25. What are the five liturgical seasons? P. 38
26. What does the priest do for us? Pp. 44, 45
27. The two main divisions of the Mass are the Liturgy of the Word and the Liturgy of the? P. 40
28. What are two things the sacrament of the Anointing of the Sick does for a person? P. 44

29. What are the two purposes of Marriage? P. 45
30. How do the 10 commandments correspond to the two great commandments? P. 47
31. Can you name the 10 commandments in order? Pp. 48-50
32. If one verbally injures someone, which commandment has been broken? P. 50
33. If one engages in pre-marital sex, which commandment has been broken? Pp. 48-50
34. What are the six commandments or precepts of the Church? Pp. 50-51
35. What are the seven vices and seven virtues? Pp. 51-52
36. Can you name the seven physical and the seven spiritual works of mercy from memory? Pp. 54-55
37. What is prayer? P. 57
38. What are the four main purposes of prayer? P. 58
39. What are the three answers we can get for our prayers? P. 59
40. Can you pray the "Our Father", "Hail Mary", "Apostles' Creed", and "Act of Contrition" from memory? Pp. 59-60
41. How many of the mysteries of the Rosary can you name from memory? Pp. 63-64